The Real Enid Blyton

The Real Enid Blyton

Nadia Cohen

PEN & SWORD
HISTORY

First published in Great Britain in 2018 by
PEN & SWORD HISTORY
An imprint of
Pen & Sword Books Ltd
Yorkshire - Philadelphia

ISBN 978 1 52672 203 4

A CIP catalogue record for this book is
available from the British Library

Typeset in Geniies IT & Services Private Limited, INDIA
Printed and bound by TJ International Ltd, Padstow, Cornwall

Pen & Sword Books Ltd incorporates the Imprints of Aviation, Atlas, Family History,
Fiction, Maritime, Military, Discovery, Politics, History, Archaeology, True Crime,
Transport, The Praetorian Press, White Owl, Seaforth Publishing and Frontline
Publishing.

For a complete list of Pen & Sword titles please contact
PEN & SWORD BOOKS LTD
47 Church Street, Barnsley, South Yorkshire, S70 2AS, England
E-mail: enquiries@pen-and-sword.co.uk
Website: www.pen-and-sword.co.uk

For Harry and Felix

Contents

Introduction

She is the most prolific children's author in history, yet Enid Blyton is also the most controversial. She was a complex, troubled and truly remarkable woman who wrote almost eight-hundred books in an extraordinary career spanning forty years, but even her notoriously razor sharp mind could never have predicted the enormous global audience she would eventually reach. Now, fifty years after her death, Enid remains a true literary phenomenon. With book sales soaring way over 600 million, she easily outranks all her rivals, and having survived backlash, scandals and slurs that threatened to ruin her reputation she is still among the most popular authors in the world today.

For years parents, teachers, librarians and critics have lobbied against Enid's books, complaining that they are too simplistic, repetitive and littered with racist, sexist and snobbish undertones. Indeed, some of her stories do feature racially offensive terms which are considered unacceptable by today's standards, while foreign characters and the working classes were treated with a distain that often horrifies modern readers. It has also been repeatedly suggested that she simply put her famous signature to stories churned out by a factory of writers.

The criticism baffled and stung Enid, although she famously said she was not interested in the opinion of anyone over the age of 12, and she refused to stop. Enid felt she owed it to her loyal army of young readers to keep going until she could not physically produce another word. Enid worked tirelessly until her memory failed her, typically producing an astonishing 6,000–8,000 words a day, hunched over her manual typewriter, as well as answering every piece of fan mail by hand.

She was a product of a far simpler and more innocent time than the one children see around them today. Enid created an idyllic place where her characters were given freedom to roam unsupervised for days on end, there were no adults to spoil their fun and there was not a problem that could not be fixed with a midnight feast or a glorious picnic – and of course lashings of ginger beer. Smugglers, thieves, spies and kidnappers were thwarted by fearless gangs of children who easily outwitted them and the police, while the most popular girls in the school always scored the winning goal in nail-biting lacrosse matches.

Enid was also a shrewd businesswoman whose canny understanding of marketing and merchandising opportunities was years ahead of her time. There have been very few authors who have come close to achieving the same success, and certainly very few women. Privately, she was prone to bursts of furious temper, which made her difficult to work and live with, and left her own children feeling unloved, yet she took great pains to carefully craft and guard her public image to ensure her young readers only knew of the sunny, happy world she created for them.

Behind the scenes, she wove elaborate stories to conceal her infidelities, betrayals and unconventional friendships. Enid spun a web of lies about her childhood, and never fully recovered from the collapse of her parent's marriage, and the feeling that her father had deserted her for someone he loved more. In many ways she remained that little girl who never really grew up, always terrified of being abandoned again. No man could ever measure up to the impossible standards she set, and she often felt rather disappointed by both her two husbands and daughters.

A quite infuriating and somewhat immature woman, Enid remained plagued by these insecurities and forever haunted by dark episodes in her past. She may not have been particularly likeable, and her stories may have been flawed, but her talent was undeniable and she has left a vast literary legacy to future generations of children.

Chapter One

In the long, hot summer of 1897, Thomas Carey Blyton and his wife Theresa Mary welcomed their first child, a much longed for daughter they named Enid Mary. Their bright and inquisitive baby, with a mop of dark curls, heralded the start of their glorious future together as a family. It was 11 August, Britain was celebrating Queen Victoria's Diamond Jubilee and the creative young couple had just bought their first home together – a two-bedroom flat above a shop at 354 Lordship Lane in Dulwich, South London. They modestly hoped little Enid might inherit their musical talents; they would have never dared to imagine she would become a household name across the globe.

Thomas had been born in Sheffield in 1870 when the steel industry was booming in the prosperous Yorkshire town. The fourth of seven children, he was artistically gifted and longed to be a pianist, but the overstretched family could not afford for Thomas to pursue a career in music, and instead he had little choice but to take a frustratingly steady job as a cutlery salesman. In 1896, at the age of 26, Thomas married his childhood sweetheart and they moved to London to join his two older brothers in their uncle's firm, Fisher and Nephews, selling Yorkshire cloth. At first he and Theresa enjoyed a happy marriage, and as Thomas worked his way up the family business he was being paid well and they were gradually climbing the social ladder too. Just months after Enid arrived they were able to move out of the capital to the more affluent suburb of Beckenham, into a spacious detached house in Chaffinch Road. In 1899 their son Hanly was born, and they moved again to a larger house in nearby Clockhouse Road, where three years later Enid's youngest brother Carey arrived to complete their family of five.

But there was no question that Enid would always remain Thomas' favourite child. They had forged a particularly close bond after Thomas saved his daughter's life when, at just 3 months old, she suffered a potentially fatal bout of whooping cough during a cold November night. Enid was so gravely ill that when they called the doctor out, he warned the Blytons that their sick daughter might not survive the night. But Thomas would not let his baby die. He refused to accept the solemn medical opinion and sat up all night cradling and rocking his beloved daughter to keep her warm. By the early hours, he realised the danger had passed, and as dawn broke Enid was sleeping peacefully in his arms. Enid loved hearing this story and throughout her childhood she would beg her father to recount the dramatic anecdote over and over again.

As well as sharing his sensitive nature and enjoying many of the same keen interests, Enid also looked like her father – they both had dark hair and brown eyes. Thomas was a passionate man with many hobbies including astronomy, playing the piano and banjo, watercolour painting, singing and writing poetry. He also taught himself French and German but his main interest was nature, wildlife and the outdoors, and he took every opportunity to take Enid on long walks so they could discover the countryside together. The Blytons' house in Clockhouse Road was where Enid spent most of her childhood years, with its sprawling garden where the three children could play happily for hours, and where Enid started to develop her early love of plants and flowers.

From the moment she could walk, Enid followed her father everywhere. Beckenham, which is now a London suburb, was then surrounded by unspoilt countryside, and the happy pair would disappear on long walks together for hours at a time. As they walked, Thomas would make up poems or tales of goblins and fairies for Enid, and shared his in-depth knowledge of the joy of nature and the countryside. His great passion for the subject never left her. Describing him years later, Enid said: 'He knew more about flowers, birds and wild animals than anyone I had ever met and was always willing to share his knowledge with me.' A enthusiastic gardener too, Thomas helped Enid develop her own patch of the garden when she was just five years old and encouraged her to be patient while she waited excitedly for the seeds to grow. He made a bargain with Enid, telling her: 'If you want anything badly, you have to work for it. I will give you enough money to buy your own seeds, if you earn it.' She was so determined to impress him that Enid would clean her father's bicycle until it gleamed, and carefully weeded the flowerbeds until she had earned sixpence – enough to buy herself a packet of seeds. With her father's help she planted them and monitored them each day as they grew into buds, and then flowers. It was an experience Enid would never forget.

Although she longed for a pet, Enid's house-proud mother refused to have an animal making the place untidy and Thomas would not let her keep one either, since he believed that animals should be kept in their natural surroundings. During one of her long walks, however, Enid found a lost kitten, which she brought home and called Chippy. But knowing how her parents both felt, she hid it in a garden shed and with the help of their young maid, Annie, Enid managed to keep Chippy a secret for two weeks. But one day when she rushed home from school to play with the kitten she realised that her mother had discovered her secret and it had been sent away. Enid was distraught when Annie broke the news to her, 'I was heartbroken', she said later. Instead Enid settled for playing in the garden with caterpillars which she found fascinating and later told how she liked 'feeling their funny little clingy feet' walking over her hands. But she would make up for it as an adult when she filled her homes with numerous pets of all kinds.

At home in the evenings Thomas would entertain his rapt daughter by playing his banjo, and singing songs. Music had always been his other great passion and he played well; one of his sisters had gone on to become a successful concert pianist and Thomas envied her career. As a keen amateur pianist, he hoped Enid would one day fulfil his own ambition of becoming a professional musician, and often told people how much she looked like his sister. He started giving Enid piano lessons when she was just 6-years-old, and keen to please and impress her father, she practised every day, although she never really enjoyed it, and gave up playing altogether when she left home at the age of 19.

After she was sent upstairs to bed, Enid would lie awake or crouch on the stairs listening to her father playing classical pieces including Beethoven's sonatas and grand compositions by Chopin, Liszt and Mozart until late into the night. She particularly enjoyed it when he played music by Bach, her favourite composer. Enid later recalled many occasions as a child when she would fall asleep to the sound of her father's melodic piano playing: 'I knew them by heart and now, whenever I hear those same pieces of music played, I seem to be back in my little bed, almost asleep, hearing my father playing hour after hour downstairs, all those years ago.'

Enid began her early education at a small nursery school just across the road from the family home in Beckenham, run by two sisters both called Miss Reid, who remembered Enid as a bright pupil who enjoyed reading, English and art, although she had trouble getting to grips with the logic of maths. She also sang well and had an excellent memory. Her favourite stories were *The Princess and The Goblin* by George MacDonald, *Alice in Wonderland* by Lewis Carroll and *Coral Island* by R.M. Ballantyne. Another firm favourite was Daniel Defoe's *Robinson Crusoe*, and these exotic settings started an early fascination for the mystery and excitement of islands and caves, which would feature so heavily in many of Enid's later stories.

Enid also loved it when Thomas read her poetry, as she liked the rhythm of the verses, although admitted she did not always understand the meaning of it: 'The lilt of the words and the beautiful stringing together of lines lifted my heart,' she said. 'My father used to quote poetry so often that it became part of my life.' She would also memorise facts from encyclopaedias and was given free rein to devour whatever she wanted from her father's extensive book collection which he had gradually accumulated by saving up for a 'sixpenny classic' every week.

Although Thomas was self-educated, he was an enthusiastic reader, and was utterly delighted that his daughter shared his love of reading. As Enid grew slightly older she preferred traditional stories for girls, including *Little Women* by Louisa M. Alcott and *Black Beauty* by Anna Sewell because they were about incidents and dramas involving real children, as opposed to mythical creatures which she was beginning to find terrifying. She said many years later: 'Those were real children. When I grow up I will write books about real children, I thought. That is the kind of book I like best. That's the kind of book I would know how to write.' She even began to pick up novels which had been written in French and German, with a dictionary beside her since she did not know either language.

The family were comfortably off, and decidedly middle class, but never took holidays abroad. Enid's grandparents still lived in Sheffield, and when she and her brothers were young the entire clan would gather together to spend Christmas at their uncle's house. At these large family gatherings, Enid always found herself drawn to the gregarious Irish grandmother she had been named after, Mary Ann Hanly. The well-educated daughter of a doctor, she fascinated and intrigued Enid as she entertained all the children with old folk songs and bewitching tales of leprechauns and banshees. As an adult, Enid was always sure her own gift for story telling had been inherited from her vivacious Irish ancestors.

Enid spent as little time as possible with her mother whom she found infuriatingly dull. Since Enid was her only daughter, Theresa expected her to help with domestic chores around the house and learn to cook and sew in order to prepare her for a successful married life. Theresa was extremely house-proud and imagined that Enid would grow up to be a traditional wife and mother just as she had been, but Enid had absolutely no interest in what she saw as a pointless existence of domestic servitude, and made her attitude crystal clear to her mother. Theresa was disappointed and as they started to pull in opposite directions their relationship became increasingly bitter. They grew more and more resentful of each other as Enid always felt that Theresa favoured the two boys, who were allowed to go out and play while it was seen as her duty to stay inside and help with the housework, although they had a maid. Instead, Enid would leap at any chance she got to disappear for hours with her father, and was thrilled to escape. Theresa was exasperated by how little Enid did to help her around the house, and she felt Thomas spoilt their daughter. Thomas found it increasingly difficult to cope with his wife's constant criticism, especially over the way he blatantly favoured Enid, and their marriage began to crack.

In 1907 the family moved again, to another semi-detached house, still in Clockhouse Road, and Enid started attending St Christopher's School in Beckenham. She loved the new school where she had the chance to learn French, play lacrosse and tennis and go swimming but things were not so happy at home. Thomas and Theresa continued to grow apart. Theresa had few interests beyond the children and their home, and it became clear the couple had less and less in common. As the resentment began to build up, they would fight constantly, and Enid's idyllic childhood would soon be shattered when Thomas met an intelligent woman who shared his love of music and books, which Theresa had never done. As the arguments grew increasingly fierce, all three children were distraught. Enid would try to distract her brothers with stories she made up for them, but when they were asleep she would sneak down to her usual hiding place on the stairs to listen, hoping to hear her father play the piano softly as usual. Instead, he would furiously slam on the keys in the wake of yet another one of their vicious rows. Enid was horrified by what she heard but even when the fighting was at its worst, she never imagined what was to come.

When Enid realised that her father was leaving permanently to start a new life with another woman she was shattered and utterly heartbroken. She was 13 and never recovered from the shock and the feeling that it was she and not her mother who had been rejected. Thomas moved away and set up a wholesale clothing business in London, leaving it to Theresa to explain his sudden disappearance to the devastated children. The repercussions, which even included issues with the late development of her reproductive organs, would haunt Enid forever. Enid's daughter Imogen later described Thomas as 'My mother's inspiration', adding, 'He was a cultured and attractive man as well as a stubborn one; imaginative as was his daughter.'

Without her father for company, Enid was bereft. Now there was no one to encourage her love of nature, nor her writing, piano playing or painting, she felt she had lost her teacher and her best friend. Her two younger brothers were good company and she had plenty in common with the boys, but they were unable to fill the gaping void which had suddenly opened up in her life. As far as Theresa was concerned, a divorce was out of the question and she refused her husband's requests to make their split official. Theresa was too ashamed to admit the truth to anyone and urged the children to pretend that their father's absence was only temporary. She was unable to bear the stigma of being a single mother, and could not stand the thought of having to endure other people's pity. If anyone asked after Thomas, the children were instructed that they must say that their father was simply 'away', and it suited Enid perfectly to keep it a closely guarded secret as she did not want to face up to the reality of the situation either.

Following her mother's stoic example, Enid decided she too would keep her feelings well hidden in a bid to maintain appearances that the family was fine. Even Enid's best friend Mary Attenborough did not guess the truth about what had really happened. Just like her mother, Enid seemed able to easily convince other people – and possibly even herself – that if she did not openly admit to something then it never actually happened. It was a clever psychological trick that Enid would use again and again throughout her later life.

Enid was not allowed to talk about her feelings or grieve in any way for the loss she had experienced. She could not forgive her father's betrayal, and always felt he had chosen someone else over her. Not only that, but he had left her with a mother who she thought did not care for or understand her. A remarkable talent for concealing the truth from the outside world was all that the two women had in common. Enid still stubbornly refused to be moulded into a younger version of her mother, and the more she rebelled, the more frustrated Theresa became with her difficult daughter.

Enid missed her father terribly, and although Theresa maintained sporadic contact with him he was never allowed to visit his children at home. According to Enid's daughter Gillian: 'She had lost her dearest friend; occasional meetings could never replace the happy daily companionship they had shared.' They saw each other occasionally, when he would take the children on outings to the theatre and give them expensive gifts, but their relationship was never the same again because Enid refused to go to the house he shared with his new partner. Thomas continued to send money for the children, and paid all their school fees, so from the outside it looked as if their life could continue much as it had before the split. Wanting to avoid as much scurrilous gossip as possible, the family moved house once again, along with their maid Annie. They did not go far, just to a slightly more desirable part of Beckenham, but they could make a fresh start. Enid's room on the first floor of their new three-storey house in Elm Road overlooked the large garden, but after installing a lock and knocker on the door, she hid away from the harsh realities of family life and retreated into her own private world. Theresa made sure that Enid continued to practise the piano for an hour each day and they regularly attended Elm Road Baptist Church, where she had been baptised.

Life went on but Enid would never again be as happy as she had been in the carefree days before Thomas fell in love with someone else. She could not wait to leave home, when she would tell everyone that her mother was dead.

Chapter Two

Thomas and Theresa's decision to split up when she was a child affected Enid terribly for the rest of her life. And given the devastating impact of Thomas walking out on his family, it was hardly surprising that in many of Enid's later stories the children she wrote about were torn apart from their parents. The betrayal she felt at her own father leaving at such a pivotal time in her development proved to be a trauma from which Enid would never fully recover. Instead, she started to teach herself how to become detached from the people closest to her, and was able to compartmentalise relationships in this way throughout the rest of her life. It would influence many of her future decisions and adult relationships, and clearly paved the way for the sort of writer, wife and mother Enid would eventually become. When she was finished with relationships, she simply removed people from her life without a backward glance. While there can be no doubt that Thomas was a great inspiration to his daughter in many worthwhile and educational ways, the complex emotional damage he inflicted also left deep scars that would never heal.

But despite the upheaval at home, Enid continued to thrive at St Christopher's, where she threw herself into all aspects of school life. She worked hard, had plenty of friends and played the piano exceptionally well. She enjoyed maths, despite her lack of natural ability at the subject, excelled at most sports, and particularly loved tennis and was captain of the lacrosse team. Enid was also known for being daring and brave, and the girls who boarded at the school nicknamed her 'the hairless day girl' because she was among the first to cut off her long hair and wear it shoulder length. Enid had a reputation as something of a prankster and enjoyed playing practical jokes on the staff, which she had usually learnt from her two younger brothers. Other pupils recalled Enid being very proud of a box of tricks she bought from the local toyshop. Many of her later 'jolly hockey sticks' stories about the high jinx of life at girls' schools were based on those years. As well as being popular among the other students, the staff were impressed with Enid's exemplary behaviour, and she was made head girl for her last two years at the school. She was top of the French class and when she was 16 in 1913 her teacher Madame Louise Bertraine took her abroad for the first time, to stay with her family near Lake Annecy, and the pair remained close friends for many years. She was the inspiration for Enid's warm-hearted but hot-headed character Mam'zelle Abominable in *The Twins at St Clare's*, the first book in that popular series.

Enid was very keen on drama at school too, and although she was rarely cast in school productions, she would write sketches and songs for herself to act out to entertain the other girls. She also found the time to set up a magazine called 'Dab', an acronym based on the surnames of her best friends Mirabel Davis and Mary Attenborough and herself. Enid wrote the stories, while the other two provided the poems and illustrations. The three stayed in contact throughout their time at school and delighted in sending each other secretly coded letters and poems during the holidays. Enid had always shown an early enthusiasm for writing, and started to submit her efforts to children's magazines in the faint hope they might one day be published. The rejections never put her off, and when she was 13, Enid was delighted to receive an encouraging letter from journalist Arthur Mee, author of the *Children's Encyclopaedia*, urging her to write more. She was an enthusiastic reader of his weekly magazine, and she was amazed when he told her she had a great talent for writing, and one of her poems appeared in print on the children's page of the next issue of the magazine. Mee was the first to spot Enid's potential, it was the first time she had seen her name in print and she was hooked: 'My words seemed quite different when they were printed, not written – they seemed so much more important', Enid recalled later.

Even though Theresa thought that sending off endless copies of her verses, most of which were rejected, was a waste of time, Enid persisted. Her mother said they could not afford to spend money on stamps and packaging, but Enid unexpectedly found herself being supported by her friend Mary's aunt Mabel Attenborough who also saw talent in her early on. Mabel was an artist who knew Enid well, and she was the first adult to whom she dared to confide her secret ambition to be a writer. Mabel's advice was to persevere, so Enid continued to post her poems without her mother realising. To conceal the truth she had to wake up early each morning and sneak downstairs to intercept the mail and retrieve any unwanted manuscripts before her mother discovered they had been returned. The fact that Enid was never disheartened by the steady stream of rejection letters that landed on the doormat was an early sign of her dogged determination to succeed which would serve her so well in later life. She said: 'It is partly the struggle that helps you so much, that gives you determination, character, self-reliance – all things that help in any profession or trade, and most certainly in writing'.

Enid read constantly and kept daily diaries, which she guarded fiercely, but after Theresa discovered them and read her private thoughts, Enid destroyed them all. Theresa said that instead she should be doing her piano practice or helping with domestic duties. From then on Enid avoided writing down any record of her personal feelings, and just noted her day-to-day activities instead. She clashed frequently with her mother who chose to live a puritan and suburban life, which held no interest for Enid at all. There were also battles with her brothers, although she would still make up stories for them at bedtime, just as she had done when their parents were fighting. Enid was finding the house increasingly claustrophobic, and started to spend as much time as possible at the Attenboroughs' house where she felt much more welcome, and her already resentful relationship with Theresa deteriorated drastically. Enid was frustrated by her mother only being interested in housework, and felt that she was critical of her daughter's growing passion for writing, and did nothing to encourage her. By her late teens, Enid had managed to get a few pieces of poetry published but with little sign of her earning any money from her modest literary success, both her parents were still absolutely determined that she should become a professional musician, and urged her to spend hours every day practising the piano. Enid reluctantly obeyed for a while and passed her Licentiate of the Royal Academy of Music exam and was offered a place to study at the prestigious Guildhall School of Music in London, which was exactly what her father had always wanted for his daughter.

But Enid's heart was not in music and by 1916 she was showing real signs of rebellion. When Mabel offered her the chance to take a break from her mother and join them on holiday that summer, Enid leapt at it. She had finished her final term at school and was due to take up her place at music school in London in September, but Mabel invited Enid to stay with her great friends George and Emily Hunt at their farm in Suffolk first. Seckford Hall, the Hunts' rambling fifteenth-century farmhouse just outside Ipswich, enchanted Enid from the first moment she laid eyes on it, and would prove so inspirational that it became the setting for many of her future stories. Before they set off for Suffolk, Mabel had told Enid that Seckford Hall had a secret passageway and a haunted bedroom, and Enid was thrilled by the idea. She loved life on the farm and relished the opportunity to help care for the animals. She spent long carefree days riding the Hunts' horses and walking their dogs. There were also bike rides and trips to the beach with their daughters Marjory and Ida, as well as several young army officers who were billeted at the farm. On Sunday afternoons Enid went along to help at Woodbridge Congregational Sunday School, and enjoyed herself so much that she started to contemplate working as a teacher while she carried on writing in her spare time.

It was during that summer at Seckford Hall that Enid realised what she wanted to do with her life, and she vowed to turn her back on the future that had been mapped out for her. Working with children would supply her with a constant source of information about what they liked and did not like, as well as ideas and material for stories. She had struck up a great friendship with Ida who was already a trainee teacher at Ipswich Girls' High School and, having watched Enid with the Sunday school children, admitted she was surprised at how quickly they responded to her style of teaching. Enid related to the class straight away, communicated easily and captivated them with her relaxed attitude to art and storytelling. However many stories she told the children, they were always eager for more. Enid was bursting with enthusiasm and could not wait to share all the knowledge of nature that her father had taught her as a young child. Ida suggested a career in teaching would still give her time to continue with her writing in the school holidays. It made perfect sense to Enid. After discussing the idea at length with Ida, Enid decided she would like to train to become a Froebel teacher, and investigated the possibility of starting a course in Ipswich that September. After making a few enquiries, she was offered a place as an apprentice teacher at the school's kindergarten.

She could not wait to move into Ida's lodgings and sever any last remaining family ties to her mother. But first she needed her father's permission to give up music school. Enid vowed to never abandon her dream of becoming a writer, but she realised that she needed to earn money if she was to be able to leave home. After her taste of freedom that summer in Suffolk, she never wanted to return to her mother's house again. Her father was surprised when Enid telephoned him out of the blue and begged him to sign an application form for her to attend a Froebel teaching course, but she would not take no for an answer. Eventually Thomas laughed at his daughter's typically headstrong determination, and agreed that she could try a different career path from the one he had hoped for. Enid was astounded that he agreed so readily, but Thomas was eerily reminded of what turned out to be an uncannily accurate prediction made years earlier by a phrenologist who had analysed the bumps on Enid's head when she was 8. Thomas had expected to be told that his daughter was a naturally gifted musician but after the examination, the doctor sent a report, which read: 'This child will turn to teaching as she develops. It is, and will be, her great gift.'

Thomas had never forgotten it and accepted that decisions about Enid's future were not his to make. Theresa on the other hand was furious about the unexpected change of plan, and fired off a series of angry letters to her daughter in a bid to convince her to keep pursuing a career in music as they had always intended. But Enid was obstinate and her mind was made up. Theresa was worried about what her friends would think about an unmarried girl leaving home to live alone in a strange city, so she invented another elaborate story to hide the truth again. Theresa feared that people would gossip about Enid having something to hide, such as an unplanned pregnancy, so instead she told them that while on holiday in Suffolk Enid had decided to join the Women's Land Army to help the war effort. The First World War had broken out and many young girls were helping on farms while the men were away fighting. Theresa further embellished the lie by also claiming that the Land Army had proved too tough for Enid but she was too afraid to come home and admit that her mother had been right all along.

Enid stopped responding to letters from her mother and her brothers shortly after her 19th birthday, and they had no communication at all for many years after that. Enid was glad to have Theresa out of her life at last; she threw herself into her training course in Ipswich and loved every aspect of teaching from the start. She was fascinated by the psychology of it, and was always cheerful with the children. She fitted into her new life so successfully that she described herself as 'a round peg in a round hole'. She had great respect for her lecturers on the course, Sophie Flear, Kathleen Fryer and Kathleen Gibbons, who shared her father's love of nature, and Enid excelled particularly in zoology, botany and geography. If Enid ever allowed herself a moment of homesickness or regret about cutting off her family, she never let it show. Theresa had taught her to hide her emotions well, and in any case she was too busy to dwell on the loss. Enid dismissed the idea of returning to her family at the end of term, having decided she would not be welcome there again, so during breaks from her course she went back to stay with the Hunt family at Seckford Hall or with her old chum Mary Attenborough. But her closest friends, especially Ida, suspected that Enid missed having regular contact with her family. Years later, when writing to her own daughters, Enid admitted that she had been hurt by her mother's coldness: 'You would much rather I did worry about you than not care what happened – which is what I always felt was the case with my own mother'.

While she juggled the demands of her training course, Enid kept up her writing as much as she could during the holidays and at weekends, and was often inspired by bike rides, trips to the seaside and picnics she enjoyed with Ida, who she gave the nickname 'Cap'n'. In March 1917 Enid's efforts were given a huge boost when *Nash's Magazine* agreed to print three of her poems in the following month's edition. Enid was excited but did not let the success derail her studies, and continued to focus until she completed her course in December 1919, at the age of 22, with first-class passes. She secured her first job at Bickley Park Preparatory School, a small school close to her family home in Beckenham, teaching boys between 6 and 8-years-old. She returned to Kent in the New Year but not to live with Theresa, instead moving into a small flat in the grounds of the school, after spending another Christmas with the Attenboroughs.

She only stayed at Bickley for a year, but the headmaster Richard Brandram was sorry to see her leave so soon, and wrote a glowing reference, in which he said: 'To be able to lead small boys and to understand their way is a gift given to few, but Miss Blyton has the secret.'

Chapter Three

In January 1921 Enid left Bickley to take up a new role as a private tutor to Mabel's cousin's son David Thompson, an 8-year-old boy who had missed a long period of schooling due to a bout of diphtheria. During her own holiday from school, Mabel herself had been helping David to catch up on the lessons he had missed, but she felt that Enid would be much better suited to the job. And so Enid moved in with the Thompson family to become governess to all four of their children. Her employers, Horace and Gertrude, were thrilled to welcome Enid to Southernhay, their home in Surbiton, Surrey, and she slotted happily into suburban life straight away.

As well as teaching David, Enid was also responsible for his younger brothers Brian and twins Peter and John. A neighbour's daughter Mollie Sayer also joined them for lessons, which Enid conducted either in the nursery or outside in the gardens where she preferred to spend as much time as possible. The children adored her instantly, and as word of the new arrival quickly spread around the area, several other parents living nearby soon wanted their children included in Enid's imaginative classes. Before long Enid seemed to be running a small school from the Thompson's house, and over the four years she spent at Southernhay she found herself teaching fourteen boys and girls aged between 4 and 10. Enid was delighted with her newfound popularity, and luckily the Thompsons were happy with the arrangement too. Managing lessons to suit the various age ranges was tough, but Enid rose to the challenge with her usual enthusiasm, and made sure every child in her care received equal attention. The children loved her lessons, which she filled with plenty of laughter and good humour, and she was sure to shower them all with plenty of praise and encouragement.

She preferred the children to call her Auntie Enid, rather than the more formal Miss Blyton. And whenever a child did particularly well they were allowed to choose which picture would be hung on the wall of the classroom that week – from a selection of brightly coloured posters Enid had spotted on display in a London Tube station. She covered all the basic academic subjects including maths, reading, handwriting, music and art, as well as making sure the older children learnt history, geography, French and nature studies. For one of her more memorable geography lessons Enid attached the address of the house to a hot air balloon and floated it off into the sky. They were all thrilled when somebody in Belgium returned the label a few weeks later. Together she and the children studied maps of Europe to try and work out the route the balloon must have taken before it landed. Enid also factored painting and crafts into the children's school day, teaching them how to weave baskets and make jewellery out of dried seeds.

She certainly kept the children on track academically, but Enid never forgot her great sense of fun, and on top of all her other responsibilities she also relished the opportunity to tackle sports, organising action-packed sessions of football in the winter and cricket matches in the summer months. She was hugely creative when it came to planning her timetable, and made sure she found the time each day to make up stories to tell the children, holding them spellbound, and her pupils always said her storytelling was the absolute high spot of each day. Enid would also write imaginative plays for her pupils to perform, as well as penning poems and songs which they would recite at concerts she staged for their parents and friends. She even whipped up the costumes and designed programmes to be sold at the door to raise funds for charity. Enid felt that regular nature walks were essential too, and would take the children on long rambles in the countryside, through the surrounding woods and meadows, to identify plants, insects and pond life. The children would collect specimens of butterflies, caterpillars and moths.

Enjoying family life for the first time in years, she affectionately started to call her employers Uncle Horace and Aunt Gertrude, and was always more than happy to pull her weight around the house. Once when the family's maid was unexpectedly taken ill shortly before an important business dinner party, Enid cheerfully took her place and saved the day, changing into the maid's uniform so she could wait on the guests before anyone suspected there was a problem. The family all adored Enid, and she was delighted to be among such a close-knit group, but then she received the unexpected news from her Uncle Charles that her father had died suddenly of a heart attack while out fishing on the Thames. Thomas was just 50-years-old, and his death came as a complete shock to Enid. Despite his bitter betrayal a decade earlier, Enid had stayed in touch with her father sporadically since leaving home, and although she refused to visit his new house, as she dreaded any form of contact with his new partner, from time to time they would have conversations on the telephone when he was in his London office and she occasionally met him there too. Thomas and Theresa had been separated for a long time, but never officially divorced because Enid's mother could not bear the shame, so he had to be buried as her husband and his funeral was to be held in her local church in Beckenham. The thought of facing Theresa after all that had happened was too traumatic for Enid. She still blamed her mother for driving her father away, and certainly did not want to meet the other woman he had chosen either, so Enid stayed away.

Once again, Enid could not bear the reality of what had happened, and this way she could keep Thomas alive in her mind. It may have been seen by many as a very strange decision to take, but it was actually typical of the way Enid dealt with all unpleasant or painful realities in her life. She simply avoided them. Going to the funeral that day would have meant facing her mother and brothers, and accepting that she would never see her father again. She was already something of an expert at putting difficult things to the back of her mind, and pretending they did not exist. This extraordinary level of self-control, to have the ability to relegate unwanted episodes to her subconscious, was something that her own children would admit to finding very confusing as they grew up, but it freed her mind to have such immense creative energy.

To many observers Enid's absence at the funeral was seen as evidence of startling coldness. She barely mentioned her father's death to the Thompson family, and was absolutely determined to carry on as normal, with her usual steeliness. Talking about her real feelings would have been far too painful – and embarrassing – for Enid to contemplate, and so she simply ignored them. However Thomas' death led inevitably to some brief contact with her brothers, as he had left them all some money in his will. By then Carey had joined the Royal Air Force, and Hanly had taken over the running of their father's business, although he was still living at home in Beckenham with Theresa, at their house in Westfield Road. Enid needed to make arrangements to receive her share of the inheritance, but she would only agree to meet at Thomas' office in London, still determined to avoid any encounters with her mother. She held several meetings with Carey and Hanly but Enid never told them the truth about her years away from home. She stuck to their mother's concocted story about the time she had apparently spent in the Women's Land Army; her brothers had no idea that she had actually been training to be a teacher in Ipswich. That was the last contact she would have with them until close to the end of her life. When she had weekends off or holidays from the Thompsons, Enid would spend them with Mabel Attenborough, and it was at one of her garden parties in 1919 that she happened to meet up with a former school friend called Phyllis Chase. They had lost touch since leaving St Christopher's but Phyllis was a keen artist trying to sell her illustrations, so the pair put their heads together and hatched a plan to submit Enid's stories along with Phyllis' pictures to publishers.

Both motivated to produce new work, Enid and Phyllis forged a partnership that proved successful for several years. Together they had light-hearted stories and poems published in 1921 and 1922 by a string of popular magazines including the *Bystander*, the *Londoner, Passing Show* and *Saturday Westminster Review*. Many more of their illustrated poems for children were printed in *Teacher's World*, a weekly magazine distributed to primary schools, and various other educational publications. Buoyed by their success, Enid became more determined than ever that she could definitely make a career out of children's writing. Before sending her stories off to publishers, she would usually read them aloud to the pupils at the little school at Southernhay to discover which aspects they did and did not like. While she found the girls tended to enjoy fairy stories and the boys preferred tales of daring and bravery, they all liked adventure stories, anything about animals, and of course they particularly loved Enid's jokes and silly nonsense that would make them all laugh. So Enid was always sure to pack her stories with plenty of humour and dialogue, which she knew the children wanted to hear.

Enid's big break into the publishing world came in 1922 when her first book of verse, *Child Whispers*, was published by J. Saville and Company, and she dedicated it to the four Thompson brothers, David, Brian, Peter and John. She had showed the class each of the poems to see if they approved before she submitted them. It was a small book, only twenty-four pages long, but Enid was brimming with fresh confidence. She knew this was just the start. In her introduction, Enid explained how she had decided to write the poems herself because she could not find anything better for her pupils. She added that she had done her own thorough research with children, and already had a very clear understanding of the type of plot lines and humour that delighted her young readers: 'The children of nowadays are different in many of their likes and dislikes, from the children of ten years ago.' She continued:

> The imagination must be clear and whimsical, otherwise the appeal fails and the child does not respond. As I found a lack of suitable poems of the types I wanted, I began to write them myself for the children under my supervision, taking in as many cases the ideas, humorous or whimsical, of the children themselves, as the theme

of the poems! Finding them to be successful, I continued until the suggestion was made to me that many children other than those in my own school might enjoy hearing and learning the poems. Accordingly this collection of verses is put forward in the hope that it will be a source of sincere enjoyment to the little people of the world.'

This was a sharp level of insight that would serve Enid well for the rest of her career.

Chapter Four

E nid's unique and remarkable ability to write precisely what children
wanted to read, and being able to relate to them with such empathy,
meant that her first book of poetry was a triumph. Following a spate of
glowing reviews, she was astonished to discover that children were begging
her publishers for more. Before long several more of her poems for adults
were published in the *Poetry Review* and the *Strand* magazine, and for the
first time she started to keep accounts to record her earnings – which topped
£200 in 1922 and £300 in 1923, a great deal at the time – about the price of
a small house. But Enid knew that she preferred writing for children rather
than adults.

Enid's second book, *Real Fairies*, was published at a time when the
mythical creatures were hugely popular in numerous children's poems and
stories. She had struck gold, and from that point Enid never looked back.
While in theory she was teaching children all day, in fact she was learning
from them too: 'It was the children themselves who taught me how to write.
No adult can teach you that as they can,' she explained later. In those early
days, many of her early poems featured maternal characters, and although
none of them appeared anything like Enid's own mother, perhaps it was
a sign that she had not managed to wipe Theresa from her mind quite as
successfully as she might have thought. But Enid had taught herself to be
tough, she was earning enough to be completely independent and from then
on parents tended to fade very much into the background in her stories.

In 1922 Enid enjoyed increasing success, with 120 more pieces appearing
in *Teacher's World*, including lesson plans for teachers and stories to share
with their pupils. She also had five poems published in a special edition
of the magazine which included contributions by distinguished poets
including Rudyard Kipling and Walter de la Mare. Within months Enid had
become so popular with readers of *Teacher's World* that she was given her
own regular weekly column called 'From My Window'. The amount of work
she was producing was hugely demanding and yet Enid was still teaching
full-time so she would often use incidents or anecdotes from the school
as material for her column, and was starting to become known to children

around the country long before she had any of her novels published. As well as providing a huge amount of educational material, she also edited three sets of encyclopaedias for teachers in junior and infant schools.

The relentless demands of the magazine and her day job left Enid with very little time for a social life, and although Mabel often invited her to various events and activities run by her local Baptist church, Enid showed no interest in any of the eligible men she was introduced to. Indeed, she appeared to have no interest in meeting a potential husband at all. She used every moment to write, and anyway, no man could possibly match up to her beloved father. But that changed the moment she first laid eyes on Major Hugh Alexander Pollock, a handsome Scotsman in his mid–30s who had left the army and taken up an editing role at her first publishing company George Newnes. Hugh had fought bravely with the Royal Scots Fusiliers during the First World War, and was awarded the Distinguished Service Order in 1919. After a short but successful stint as an officer in the Indian army, he moved to London where Enid, then 26, was immediately charmed when he called her in for a meeting, and found herself fascinated by his glamorous sounding background.

It was the beginning of February 1924 when Hugh received copies of her early poems and began commissioning Enid to write educational nature stories for children for the publishers. She clearly enjoyed collaborating closely with him on the new ideas he proposed to her, and Enid was smitten from their very first meeting. Fortunately, Hugh felt the same and just a few days later he suggested meeting at London Zoo to discuss his idea for a new book about animals. Enid gushed in her diary: 'Met Hugh at two. Taxied to Piccadilly Restaurant and had tea and talked til six! He was very nice. We're going to try and be real friends and not fall in love! Not yet at any rate. We are going to meet again tomorrow.'

The following day, after another walk in the park, Enid made her feelings about Hugh very clear in her diary: 'We're going to have a purely platonic relationship for three months and then see how we stand. Oh dear!' Over the next few weeks, Enid showed her usual characteristic determination and set out to make Hugh change his mind about being just friends. She wrote him a long letter sensibly explaining exactly how she felt about him. As soon as he received it, Hugh took her out for dinner in Covent Garden. Her plan was working: 'I know he loves me, but I'm not going to say I love him till he has proved himself,' she wrote.

Whether or not Enid knew at this stage that Hugh was already married is not clear, she was certainly rather naïve and idealistic when it came to the idea of romantic love. Regardless of any obstacles, Enid had decided Hugh was the one for her, and simply assumed it would all work out in the way she wanted. It quickly emerged that Hugh's first wife had actually left him for another man while he was away fighting in the war, so he was free to pursue her and just as Enid hoped the courtship developed rapidly. By the end of February the couple had fallen deeply in love, with Hugh whisking Enid out to glamorous London nightspots and restaurants she had never even heard of before. As her first proper boyfriend, this dashing and worldly older man completely swept Enid off her feet. He took her for dinner at the Strand Hotel and to her first ever dance at Prince's Restaurant in Piccadilly, although the thought of dancing in public made Enid panic slightly, so she begged Phyllis' husband to give her lessons the week before so she would not make a fool of herself. She treated herself to a fashionable new dress for the occasion, and she and Hugh danced until dawn. Just hours later she made the journey back from Beckenham into London again to spend yet more time with Hugh, but during a walk by the river that day they had their first disagreement, about who was the boss in their relationship.

Ahead of her time and exceptionally capable of taking care of herself, Enid was not going to be defined by the typical roles of the day, but let Hugh believe he was in charge for the time being: 'Hugh wouldn't give way an inch and I loved him for it,' she wrote afterwards. 'I think I do want him to be master.' That disagreement was an early indication of what lay in store for the couple. Plenty more rows were to follow, some even dragging on for several days, usually sparked by Hugh's jealous streak, as Enid's earnings far outweighed his and she made it clear that he was surplus to requirements. Usually he would be the one to apologise and gave Enid lots of little presents to make amends.

But in the early days they were both besotted and spent as much time together as they could spare, given they both had demanding full-time jobs. There were trips to the cinema and theatre, and whenever they could not be together, there were endless telephone calls and lengthy letters exchanged between the couple too. Energetic Enid even admitted in her private diary that she was 'dreadfully tired' but was determined to keep up with her new boyfriend who also enjoyed taking her on long, bracing walks in the countryside. He shared her passion for nature, and she related some of their excursions in her column, describing Hugh as her 'companion' although eagle-eyed editors at *Teacher's World* soon noticed how much more 'whimsical' her writing was starting to become. By the beginning of April, after a three-month courtship, Enid and Hugh decided to give each other matching signet rings as a mark of their devotion, but the day they were due to exchange the rings, Hugh was summoned to a tense meeting with Mabel's Uncle Ralph. Ralph Thompson was a solicitor who had discovered that Hugh was still married when he noticed that his divorce case was due to be heard in court. Ralph sternly reprimanded Enid for being seen out with Hugh in public. After all, she was still living under his roof and Ralph was concerned about his own reputation if he were seen to be condoning Hugh's infidelity.

Hugh was mortified, but with her usual pragmatism, Enid saw the positive side of this potentially embarrassing situation and pointed out that the imminent legal proceedings meant that Hugh would soon be free. It may have been extremely awkward for Hugh, but Enid simply glossed over the matter in her diary with a brisk lack of emotion. There was no doubt in her mind that they would be married as soon as they had the chance, and Enid was certainly not the sort of woman to let a few little things like the slow pace of the divorce courts, or even a pesky ex-wife, stand in her way.

That Easter she left her job, explaining that she would need to go before the end of the school year in order to be free for her impending marriage, regardless of the fact that Hugh had not actually proposed yet. She said cheerful goodbyes to the family, and appeared to show little remorse that the school could not continue without her, and would have to close its doors as soon as she left. She was making plenty of money from her many writing commissions, so her financial motivation for teaching was gone too. A few of the pupils tried to keep in touch for a while, but once she had moved on mentally, Enid closed that chapter of her life and hardly ever referred to the Thompsons or Southernhay again. The closest she ever came to publicly discussing this time was in an entry for the 1938 edition of the reference book *Who's Who*, in which Enid admitted that she taught in 'an experimental school'. Again, she displayed that remarkable capacity to bury wistful memories completely, and that period was the last time she had any close relationship with children. Of course she loved the idea of children, in abstract and at a distance, but she fostered no more meaningful bonds with any individuals – including her own children. Much later her daughter Imogen would reveal how she was never as kind to her own children as she was to others she did not know: 'As one of her two children who should have been the closest to her of all, I saw her only as a distant authority, a clever person, a strong and imaginative actress on the little stage of my life but never, or almost never, a mother.'

But close to the end of her life in 1962 at a time when she was frequently confused about what time period she was living in, Enid had an uncharacteristic moment of nostalgia after receiving an unexpected letter from her former pupil Brian Thompson. She replied to him, saying: 'Your letter recalled the dear old days at Southernhay, where I was so happy with your family and loved you children so much! I think it was the foundation of all my success. It was one of the happiest times of my life when I had that little school.'

In 1924, Enid drew a line under her teaching career, absolutely convinced she was making the right decision, and refused to allow herself even a moment of self-doubt. Royalties were already coming through from her first book sales, and teachers around the country were using her stories, songs and poems in their own classrooms. She would receive regular letters of thanks from staff and pupils alike. On top of her writing success, Enid was also busy with her budding romance with Hugh and they spent Easter together on their first trip away, to Seaford in Sussex. Although it was frowned upon for her to be seen with a married man, Hugh's divorce proceedings had officially begun, so the couple started to look at flats and rings, and within weeks he had proposed. On the night of their engagement she wrote in her diary: 'It's been a heavenly evening and it's so simply lovely to be engaged to my darling, darling Hugh and have his ring on my finger.' The engagement was formally announced in the pages of *Teacher's World*, and they set about planning the wedding for 28 August. Hugh moved into lodgings nearby so that they could see each other every day in the run up to the low-key ceremony, which was held at Bromley Register Office. Mabel and her parents were the only guests, not a single member of either the bride or groom's families attended the wedding, just as Enid had not attended her brother Hanly's wedding two months earlier. There were no public announcements of the wedding itself, and Enid did not even record the event in her diary. She explained to her friends afterwards that Hugh did not want his colleagues at Newnes to think he was being unprofessional by marrying one of their authors. Enid did not care about the lack of fuss, she was far from a traditional blushing bride. She just wanted the formalities over so that they could be a respectable couple at last, and move into their new top-floor flat overlooking the River Thames in Chelsea, between the Embankment and King's Road.

Despite now being Mrs Pollock, it was very much business as usual for Enid. While many women at that time would traditionally stop working as soon as they were married, Enid was certainly not going to let it interfere with her ambitious career plans. She made it clear that she would not be changing her professional name, and would continue to write as Enid Blyton. Hugh was completely supportive of her unconventional decision, and encouraged her writing as much as he could, helping out and advising her over contracts and royalties. Following a brief honeymoon in Jersey, Enid was straight back to her desk. In 1925 she managed to earn an impressive £1,200 for her year's work, which included a hefty £500 advance for her forthcoming reference book *Teacher's Treasury*. The children's stories which Hugh had commissioned, *The Enid Blyton Book of Fairies* and *The Zoo Book*, were published in October 1924 and were both great successes. Enid was becoming rather famous, and *Teacher's World* promoted her to their most prolific writer and twice a month she had a full-page feature called 'Nature Notes', which she also illustrated herself. The columns were later collated into a prize-winning book, and of course she continued to flourish at Newnes. *The Enid Blyton Book of Bunnies*, featuring the adventures of naughty rabbits Binkle and Flip trying to be good, was published in 1925, and many people thought it was about Enid and Hugh's early days as a newly married couple.

She was producing thousands of words of fiction a day, as well as replies to her rapidly increasing bags of fan mail. Enjoying her first taste of success, initially Enid seemed happy to be working alone in their new apartment in London, but soon she was longing to spend more time in the countryside. Hugh, who had grown up in rural Ayrshire, was also keen to leave London life behind, so at the start of 1925 she started house-hunting. Once again, Enid found herself being drawn back to her roots in Beckenham. On a quiet street they found the perfect place to begin the next chapter of their lives – in the appropriately named Elfin Cottage.

Chapter Five

For Enid, moving into what she thought of as their first proper home was hugely exciting. Shortlands Road in Beckenham was close enough to the station for Hugh to commute easily to his office in London every day, but still gave them the rural environment they both craved. The house was just 10 minutes walk from Mabel's home, and Enid attempted to throw herself into a new life of domestic bliss. Of course, as her mother had discovered to her cost, Enid was not a natural housewife and struggled with the many new challenges of running a home. Unfortunately, she was a terrible cook, but enjoyed shopping for furniture and picking out curtains and cushions. She was much happier when it came to the garden, she knew just how she wanted it all to look, and immediately set about drawing up detailed plans and planting hundreds of bulbs and flowers with great enthusiasm. She often wrote about the birds and wildlife that visited the garden of Elfin Cottage, and used it as inspiration for many new stories and poems. She was an expert ornithologist and would feed birds crumbs from her hands, among her favourite visitors to the garden were a friendly jackdaw and a magpie she called Jackie and Maggie, as well as a toad she named Terence. Enid was often sent seeds and cuttings from loyal readers of her columns 'Nature Notes' and 'From My Window'. In 1926 Newnes published her *Bird Book* which contained fifteen expertly researched chapters, based on her daily diaries which recorded all the birds that came into the garden.

Enid and Hugh spent most evenings working together in the garden, and they hired a gardener named Barker to help dig the flowerbeds and a pond for goldfish, surrounded with crazy paving, which was discovered many decades later by the new owners. There was also a vegetable plot, and she was thrilled that they finally had the space for their first dog, a black and white fox terrier named Bobs. He was immediately a huge hit with her readers, and in September 1929 she was given another regular page in *Teacher's World*, called 'Letters from Bobs', which proved to be such a popular feature that the letters were collected and published together in a successful book of the same name.

Enid was a well-respected figure in the education industry, and her teaching guides including *Teacher's Treasury*, a three-volume book, and the six-volume *Modern Teaching* were considered indispensible handbooks by schools around the country. They were advertised with the slogan: 'Let Enid Blyton help you in your work' and received glowing reviews from experts and head teachers who found her practical tips and advice invaluable. As well as providing lesson plans, she also wrote a series of dances, plays and songs for children to perform. She included sections on history, geography, nature studies, science, art, housecraft and needlework, which were sometimes written by experts but commissioned and edited by Enid. Over the following years various extra editions were bought out for infants and senior school pupils. She also took over the editorship of a children's magazine called *Sunny Stories for Little Folks*, again published by Hugh's company Newnes, and later became *Enid Blyton's Sunny Stories*. Each instalment would finish at an exciting point, often with characters in an awkward or dangerous situation or on the verge of making an important discovery, and these cliff-hangers guaranteed children would want to buy the next issue of the magazine.

Enid also finished a series of musical plays called *The Play's The Thing* and a storybook called *Let's Pretend*. *Teacher's World* continued to publish as many of her contributions as they could, including special supplements for her in-depth interviews with other much-loved children's authors including A.A. Milne. Recalling the moment she met the famous Winnie-the-Pooh author, Enid wrote: 'He is just like you would expect him to be. Tall, good-looking, with friendly eyes and a whimsical mouth that often smiles. He is natural and unaffected, and is diffident to an astonishing degree, considering how suddenly and generously fame has come to him.' In another special supplement, Enid herself was interviewed at home by Hugh, who asked his wife a question he had apparently been 'meaning to ask for a long time'. He wanted to know why 'she must work so hard when she had a husband, home, happiness and peace?' Enid replied: 'So long as one child tells me that my work brings him pleasure, just so long shall I go on writing.' In his piece Hugh described her as: 'A slim, graceful, childish figure with a pair of merry brown eyes,' adding that she was a 'young understander of that which is the hearts of all helpless things, be they children, animals, birds or flowers'.

'I'd love to write a novel about children,' Enid told him. 'And the jolly, happy things of life.' The intimate nature of the article boosted her popularity even further, and at Christmas 1927 she received more than 500 letters, 200 cards and over 100 presents from children and teachers all over the world. Hugh finally managed to convince her to start using a typewriter, after surprising her with one as a gift, although she was reluctant to use the new-fangled contraption, and struggled with typing at first. But she was determined to master it, and within a few months she was churning out an astonishing 6,000 words a day, sticking to a regular daily routine of seeing Hugh off to the station at 8 o'clock every morning then working flat out in the dining room or garden with the typewriter balanced on her knee. She made a point of always putting the typewriter away when her husband returned from work in the evening, so they could have dinner together or go to the cinema. She very rarely worked at the weekend, and as little as possible when they were on holiday. But Enid still insisted on replying to all her fan mail by hand, since she felt that the children who wrote to her were her close friends.

Even though neither she nor Hugh knew how to drive, Enid showed that same determination when he bought their first car, a small red Rover, and booked them both lessons. Once she had mastered the skill, Enid replaced 'From My Window' with a new column called 'Letters To Children' in which she gave detailed accounts of her amusing excursions in the car, including a particularly disastrous trip up to the Scottish highlands, plagued with punctures. After that the couple stayed closer to home, usually preferring to take their holidays in Dorset or Sussex. And although they argued like most couples, often about how Enid did not get along with Hugh's mother, in those early days they appeared very happy and had affectionate nicknames for each other – she called him 'Bun', and he called her 'Little Bunny'. For the first time since her father had left, Enid felt secure and loved. It was an idyllic time as they showered each other with gifts, and made time to play games like cricket in the summer and built snowmen together in the winter. And on their second wedding anniversary Enid wrote in her diary: 'I am glad I married Hugh and I wouldn't be unmarried for worlds. He is such a perfect dear.'

But the honeymoon phase was not to last, and gradually it became clear that everything was not quite as perfect as it may have seemed. There were tempestuous times for the couple as they longed for a baby but Enid was starting to fear that she might never get pregnant. By 1928, almost all of Enid and Hugh's friends had children, and yet they were unable to conceive. Mary Attenborough was married with a young son, who visited regularly, and her brother Hanly had become the father of a little girl, Enid's niece Yvonne. She was constantly writing for children and yet did not have her own. Eventually Enid made an appointment to be examined by a gynaecologist who diagnosed she had an unusually underdeveloped uterus, about the same as a young girl of 12 or 13. It seemed she had stopped developing physically the moment her father walked out, possibly because of the shock.

But Enid was determined to have the baby she longed for and insisted on pioneering fertility treatment to rectify the problem. It was rare at the time, but the doctor prescribed several weeks of daily hormone injections, but when they were still unable to conceive, Enid decided to find herself a new project and announced they would be moving house. She had discovered that a major new road was to be built close to Elfin Cottage, and unable to stand the thought of having their tranquillity disturbed, Enid asked her readers to send details of any properties they knew of for sale. She was inundated with possibilities, and was delighted when she found a much larger thatched cottage in Bourne End, Buckinghamshire. Enid also asked her readers to suggest new names for the house, and they came flooding in – including Pixie Cottage, Ding Dong Bell Cottage, Fairy Cottage and Brownie Cottage. But when they moved, in August 1929, she and Hugh decided to keep the original name, Old Thatch. It was a former pub where the famous highwayman Dick Turpin was said to have stayed once, and it was claimed that the ghosts of his horses could still be heard. Enid was thrilled that the garden was 'about nine times as big' as the one they had at Elfin Cottage, and included an orchard of fruit trees, a small wood, a brook, lily pond and a kitchen garden. As well as her 'Letters to Children', Enid also continued writing regular columns – 'Enid Blyton's Children's Page' and 'Letters from Bobs', in which she pretended to be their pet dog. Bobs' letters were an instant hit, and were soon being sold to readers in small booklets which she and Hugh published privately and dispatched from their new home, costing threepence each. Within the first week of the letters being published, sales exceeded 10,000 copies, and readers begged for more.

In the meantime Enid was also working on adapting various regular series from the magazine to be later published as books by Newnes, including *Tales from Arabian Nights*, *Tales of Ancient Greece*, *Knights of the Round Table* and *Stories from World History*. By far the most popular series was a highly detailed weekly course of seasonal nature study called *Round the Year with Enid Blyton*. Each of the forty-eight lessons included imaginative methods of teaching pupils about weather patterns, how to make bird tables or plant bulbs, and the magazine editor was inundated with letters of thanks and praise from teachers who credited her with transforming classrooms across Britain. Until then many lessons had involved learning by rote, but Enid encouraged teachers to be more practical than ever. Staff and pupils at hundreds of schools felt that they knew Enid personally, were familiar with her home and garden, not to mention her husband and collection of pets which now included pigeons, a tortoise, a Siamese cat called Bimbo and fox terriers Topsy and Sandy – who later mated with Bobs and had several puppies. But Bobs always remained by far the most popular, and was quite famous in his own right. She created The Tail Waggers Club for dogs and their owners, and Enid had picture postcards of Bobs printed, and sometimes sent out as many as 100 a day without the help of a secretary. The amount of letters and parcels – which often included bunches of flowers and insects – soon meant that the small Post Office at Bourne End had to allow time for Thatch Cottage to receive its own special delivery every day. They often received letters addressed simply to 'Enid and Bobs'.

Although she must have been devastated when Bobs died, Enid refused to accept he had gone. She had ignored various warnings from their loyal gardener Dick Hughes that the dog was ill, and revealed a chilling level of ambition when Bobs died of old age in November 1935 by refusing to bring an end to the 'Letters from Bobs'. Even when Hugh buried the dog in the garden, Enid would not allow him to mark the grave as she hated to be thought of as sentimental or nostalgic in any way. Unable to face up to the sad news, she continued to write cheerful columns about what naughty tricks Bobs had been up to that week. Enid carried on imagining he was alive because, as with so many unpleasant things in her life, she preferred to pretend it never happened. She wrote in Bobs' voice until 1945, ten years after he had died.

Enid was never overwhelmed by her popularity, and took great delight in opening every package herself. She told her readers that they had a greater chance of a reply if they wrote together as classes or schools, rather than individuals, and so she was soon receiving giant envelopes stuffed with anything from twenty to fifty letters from fans. She was so strict with herself about responding to readers, that she put a penny in a box for Great Ormond Street Children's Hospital in London every time she failed to reply. That box full of coins turned out to be the first of many donations she would make over the years. At one stage she asked readers to donate silver foil for the hospital to sell, and within days she was swamped with rolls of paper which she then had to parcel up and forward on to London, one of many administrative tasks which Enid chose to tackle herself. The hospital had made a nationwide appeal but, perhaps unsurprisingly, Enid's readers were by far the biggest donors. Every time she mentioned an organisation, charity or appeal she supported, it was flooded with responses. She wrote about how impressed she was by the work of an anti-litter organisation called the

Pick Up Paper Society, which then received so many new applications that the factory which made its badges had to work overtime to keep up with the massive demand from all around the world.

Life was much busier for Enid in Bourne End than it had been in Elfin Cottage. The Pollocks were climbing the social ladder and could employ several servants including a number of maids, a cook and a full-time gardener and chauffeur to help her cope with the house. The gardener, Dick Hughes, and his new wife moved into a small cottage in the grounds where four of their children were born during the nine years he spent working for Enid at Old Thatch. Most of the maids did not receive such favourable treatment from Enid however, and she sacked one young girl for going out with a friend who had developed scarlet fever. Enid was furious that the maid might be putting the family at risk, called her a fool and insisted she was quarantined in her room for a week before telling her to leave. Although the maid never actually contracted scarlet fever herself, Enid had no sympathy.

She and Hugh began to make new friends in the area, and were persuaded to join local tennis and bridge clubs, and found themselves in demand at cocktail parties and dinners. But if she had her way Enid would rather spend her evenings reading historical novels or romances, or completing the *Daily Telegraph* crossword puzzle, although she never won the much-coveted book token which was sent out as a prize. She also had talents for watercolour painting and embroidery too, all of which she would do to relax when she finished working. By the autumn of 1930 they had enough money to travel abroad for the first time, and Enid told her readers all about a rather exotic cruise they took to the Canary Islands, unable to resist giving a geography lesson with a map of their ship's route from the docks at Southampton: 'I am going to tell you exactly where I am going and you can find all the places,' she wrote to her excited readers. She went on to provide regular updates while on her travels, via Air Mail. At least four columns were devoted to her trip aboard the *Stella Polaris*, which included visits to Madeira, Tenerife, Seville, Gibraltar and Casablanca. She even managed a letter from Bobs about his joy at having Enid home again at the end of the holiday.

Although Enid said the holiday had been 'glorious' and used it for many of the settings of her future stories, she preferred England, Dorset in particular for holidays and only ever went abroad once more in her life. A huge stack of mail had piled up in her absence, and Enid wanted to reply to as much of it as possible, although she had felt unwell since returning home.

A few weeks later her doctor confirmed that Enid was finally pregnant with their first baby.

Chapter Six

News of her pregnancy should have been cause for celebration but Enid was far too busy with her writing to consider taking time off or to make plans for the new arrival. Although she had endured months of hormone injections, she appeared far from jubilant and her diary entry was as brisk as ever: 'The doctor came and examined me and said for certain I am pregnant, just about three months. I am so glad. That explains the horrid sickness.'

Enid was 34 by then, which was considered late to be having a baby in those days, so doctors advised her that the baby could be at risk. Enid had no intention of easing up on her heavy workload, but once it had been confirmed that the baby was definitely due in July 1931, Hugh did manage to persuade her to take a short break from her typewriter. He took her to a hotel in Bournemouth for a few days away over the Easter holidays, but instead of using the opportunity to rest, Enid set about making baby clothes and embroidering linen for the nursery instead. She confided to friends that she was rather nervous about the birth, but when the day came it went very smoothly and after just five hours of labour, Gillian Mary Pollock was born in the early hours of 15 July. Enid described her as 'a lovely child', adding: 'Hugh is delighted. Baby sucked as soon as she was put to the breast.' Hugh already had two children from his previous marriage, but Gillian was his first daughter and he was ecstatic at her arrival. Enid however would not tolerate any fuss, and sent him back to his desk the same afternoon.

Enid had sensibly prepared several weeks' worth of her *Teacher's World* columns in advance, so she could take some time off following Gillian's birth, which conveniently coincided with the school holidays. But she could not wait to tell her readers about the new arrival, and on 26 August she wrote:

A lovely new pet has come to Old Thatch. Some of you have heard the news already, but I know a great many of you have not, because the pet arrived in the holidays. You can have three guesses – what is it? I am sure you are nearly all wrong, so I must tell you. Well, the new pet is a little baby girl! As many of you know I am not really

Miss Blyton because I am married, and I am so pleased that a baby has come to live with me, because you all know how much I love boys and girls – and it is lovely to have one that really belongs to me and not some other mother and father.

Gillian's arrival was also the subject of Bobs' letter to the children, with the dog revealing his supposed views about the latest addition to the family: 'I do hope the Mistress won't forget to love me, her oldest pet, now.' As soon as Enid announced the happy news to the public, she was swamped with presents for the baby but felt obliged to apologise for not sending thank you notes as promptly as she would have liked because 'the new pet' was taking up rather more time than she had anticipated.

She pretended to the outside world that she was blissfully happy, of course, but Enid struggled with a newborn and even though Gillian had been weaned on to a bottle within a month, there was still not enough time to keep up with her writing commitments so she hired a full-time nanny. Her old friend Phyllis Chase recommended a nanny called Betty who had helped take care of her own son Barry, and Enid immediately moved the young girl into Gillian's nursery, where she slept every night too, to take full charge of the baby. Enid was delighted with the new arrangement, which meant she could get back to work, and by the start of 1932 she was spending barely an hour a day with her daughter, but instead had thrown herself into her most exciting project yet, her first full-length novel for adults.

It was an entirely new challenge for Enid and she approached it with her usual energetic determination. While she scarcely mentioned little Gillian in her diary entries for January, she recorded updates on the new book almost every day. She started work on the novel on 6 January and by the 15th Enid said she was already a third of the way through, often writing a staggering 7,000 words a day. On 5 February she announced: 'Finished my novel! About 90,000 words.' Enid raced up to London for a meeting with her literary agent A.P. Watt and confidently handed him the first draft of *The Caravan Goes On*, certain she had a best seller on her hands. But when he returned the manuscript two weeks later, saying it was unpublishable, Enid was stunned. It had been many years since anything she had written had been turned down, but rather than waste any more time and effort struggling over it, she hid her disappointment and vowed she would only ever write for children after that.

With her usual pragmatic approach, Enid recycled the story and several of its strongest grown-up characters in a later children's book called

Mr Galliano's Circus. Life at the circus was something that appealed greatly to Enid, particularly the animals, the excitement and the unusual characters, so she found herself writing about them frequently. Trips to the circus had been popular sources of children's entertainment when she was growing up, and over the course of her career, twelve of Enid's books had the word circus in the title, and there were trips to watch the circus as special treats in many of her other stories. Circus folk were usually depicted as dirty with rough and ready manners, but they were kind, honest and cheerful.

If Enid found the lack of interest in *The Caravan Goes On* hurtful in anyway, she did not show it. It was a setback but only a minor one, and in any case she was quite distracted at the time by upheaval at home. Gillian fell out of her cot shortly after her first birthday, and Enid blamed the accident entirely on Betty, who was fired, even though the baby was not hurt. Enid decided to look after her daughter herself from then on. She often wrote about Gillian in her columns, usually referring to how much the child enjoyed caring for all their animals which by then also included a rapidly expanding menagerie of chickens, ducks and turkeys. Enid also took great delight in telling her readers about various other misfortunes including flooding, her own head colds and ear infections, and even a time when an infestation of rats meant she and Gillian had to move out while the house was fumigated.

Hugh was busy too, as Enid was not the only high-profile author he was managing at the time. He was also working with future Prime Minister Winston Churchill on a series of political essays that were bound into volumes called *The World Crisis*. Churchill was out of office and in the political wilderness at the time, but Hugh found it fascinating working alongside him as he warned Britain about the potential dangers of Hitler's relentless campaign for power. Like Hugh, Churchill had seen at first hand the impact of the First World War, and the two men had lengthy challenging political discussions during Hugh's many visits to Chartwell, Churchill's estate in the Kent countryside. Hugh thoroughly enjoyed their meetings, but gradually he found that having to relive some of his own army experiences was taking its toll. Hugh very rarely talked to Enid about the horrors he had witnessed as a soldier, but when Churchill asked for his personal views and to share memories of friends he had lost in the trenches, Hugh could not refuse. He was fiercely patriotic and had great admiration for the politician, but he often returned home to Enid both physically and mentally exhausted, usually stopping off at the pub on the way.

Hugh found Churchill's absolute certainty that another war was on the horizon frightening and worrying. And if he arrived back at Old Thatch to find that Enid had arranged a drinks party or a game of bridge, he would make his excuses, leaving her to attend alone. Hugh was tense, stressed and short-tempered. Most evenings he was tired and silent, and it was clear he had been drinking heavily. Enid did not want to admit the extent of the problem, but the gardener Dick Hughes felt obliged to point out to Enid that he felt sure that his boss was on the verge of some kind of nervous breakdown.

After a while Enid could no longer ignore her husband's fragile state of mind, nor his heavy drinking binges. It was hard for her to face up to problems, but she did once make reference to the toll it was taking, by writing in her *Teacher's World* column: 'Gillian's daddy has been working very hard and I want to take him as far from London as possible.' She insisted on a holiday to Scotland, without the baby, in a bid to take Hugh's mind off work, but the inevitability of war loomed large and was constantly on his mind. He spent the first day in Edinburgh working and in the middle of the trip he had to fly back to London on urgent business. Enid was worried and in another bid to help him unwind, Enid presented her husband with a drum kit for his birthday. Given the fact that Enid hated loud noises, and was often telling Gillian off for being too noisy, it clearly showed how very worried she was about Hugh's fragile mental state. Enid tried not to mind when he played it for hours on end in a bid to relax. He was working longer and longer hours, not returning home until late into the evening, and at one stage they saw so little of each other that Enid resorted to writing him letters.

Although she kept herself busy taking care of Gillian, whom she had nicknamed 'Dilly', gardening and of course writing, Enid was fearful of Hugh's growing anxiety. By the summer of 1934 most of his time was consumed with editing new volumes of *The Great War*, and matters were not helped at home by a long visit from his mother whom Enid then had to drive all the way home to Ayr in Scotland, as Hugh was not well enough to do it himself. She suggested another holiday, this time to a house she had rented near the beach on the Isle of Wight, and the change of scene appeared to agree with Hugh who finally had a chance to relax, and on their return Enid discovered that she was pregnant once more.

They hoped the baby might be a boy, and despite their disappointment when Enid suffered an early miscarriage, by the start of 1935, she was expecting again. And, just as before, she refused to let another pregnancy slow her down, and her workload was just as intense as it had ever been. Eight new children's books were due for publication that year, she was still writing her weekly *Teacher's World* columns, editing *Sunny Stories* magazine and contributing features every month to *Country Letter* and *The Nature Lover* magazine, and she was editing a guide called *Birds of Wayside and Woodland.*

Enid was furious when her due date came and went in early October with no sign of the baby, as she had planned her delivery meticulously, and certainly did not like not being in full control at all times. She was angry at being made to wait, and the household staff were all relieved when Imogen Mary Pollock finally put in an appearance on 27 October, weighing a healthy 8lb 6oz. Just as when she had given birth to Gillian, Enid did not want any fuss and taking maternity leave was out of the question. She described Imogen in her diary as 'a sweet little baby' and *Teacher's World* readers were duly informed that 'another new pet' had arrived at Old Thatch. Even many years later their second daughter remained firmly convinced that her mother preferred Gillian, who was 'a serene and beautiful child', and felt that she always remained the favourite of Hugh's four children.

Having two small children to take care of was an impossibly daunting task for Enid and she simply did not have time so hired a nanny to care for the children, a charming unmarried woman named Dorothy Gertrude Richards. Dorothy had trained at St Thomas' Hospital in London, and had handled plenty of awkward patients in the past. Enid liked her immediately, but Dorothy was already in great demand and was not able to start her new job until some weeks after the baby had been born. In her place the agency sent a nanny called Miss Herbert, but she did not last long and was soon sacked for apparently making up bottles to the wrong strength and risking the baby's health. Enid had no intention of breastfeeding and was annoyed at the nurse's insistence that she should try.

Enid was so relieved when Dorothy finally arrived that the pair immediately struck up a friendship that became so close that Hugh began to feel surplus to requirements. Dorothy was entirely responsible for Imogen's care, and accepted Enid's somewhat surprising lack of maternal instincts calmly and sympathetically, encouraging her to get back to work in the hope it would prevent her from building up feelings of resentment towards the baby. Enid was delighted by Dorothy's calm and non-judgemental attitude and they quickly discovered that they had a great deal in common. They were the same age and found they had plenty to talk about that did not involve the baby. 'The new nurse is sweet,' Enid wrote in her diary: 'The new nurse is awfully nice and I like her very much.' Although Dorothy had to leave at the end of November, having already committed to another job, their friendship was well established and the pair kept in frequent contact, with constant telephone calls, letters and visits to one another. She promised to return as soon as she could.

The Pollock family was complete, but Enid and Hugh were far from happy: 'By the time I was born in 1935, circumstances in my parents' life had changed,' Imogen reflected years later. 'Stresses were appearing in the marriage. Possibly she was beginning to show the selfishness that so often characterises creative people as they find that their work cannot take second place to other people's needs. I suspect also that she was beginning to outgrow my father.'

Hugh was furious that Enid had been asking Dorothy to proofread early drafts of her work instead of him, and hated all the private jokes the two women shared together. He started drinking far more than usual and was often depressed. Enid did her best to ignore his moods, and turned a blind eye when he flirted with other women as he was prone to do, especially when he had been drinking. But she could no longer ignore his insecurities nor his vulnerable side, and a mental weakness that left her feeling unable to rely on him in the same way. In the early stages of their relationship, Hugh had been very much in charge and she had counted on his strength and guidance in all matters. But she had little sympathy for his physical failings, and when she realised that he was unable to protect her or make her feel secure in the same way as before, there was a definite shift in the nature of their marriage.

Dorothy soon returned to Old Thatch, and Enid found herself taking long walks with her new friend, opening up emotionally in a way she had never done before and discussing intimate affairs of the heart. Enid would usually only spend an hour a day with the girls, but when Dorothy was there she changed her rigorous working schedule to spend the entire morning with them. Enid usually produced between 5,000 and 6,000 words a day, but writing was not a priority when her friend was visiting. Enid also spent so many evenings with Dorothy that she noticed that her possessive husband Hugh was becoming 'very grumpy'.

Their marriage never really recovered after Enid met Dorothy.

Chapter Seven

Hugh resented Dorothy's intrusion into their domestic arrangements, and could not help but notice how his wife had started to rely on her new friend, rather than him. Enid's earnings already far outstripped his, which left Hugh feeling rather superfluous, and he felt she did not give him any credit for commissioning the books in the first place.

During one of their many intimate discussions Dorothy revealed that she had converted to Catholicism. Enid was intrigued and rather jealous of the comfort it gave Dorothy, and her interest led to a series of long heartfelt letters exchanged between the two women about spirituality and the nature of their beliefs. Having been raised a Baptist, Enid said that religion frightened and depressed her, and she saw God as a threatening and angry masculine figure. But for a time Enid began to look at Catholicism as a religion she might adopt. She was interested once again in prayer, as she had been as a child, when she and her father shared a spiritual connection, and said prayers together every night.

It was rare for Enid to open herself up in such a frank way, but she cared deeply about what Dorothy thought of her and sought her opinion on a wide variety of subjects. She felt able to expose her most personal thoughts to Dorothy and could be searingly honest for the first time in her life. She had never experienced a friendship anything like it. Dorothy was said to be rather masculine, and often dressed in a formal shirt and tie. Enid was not overly feminine or vain, she never wore high heels or the latest fashions, but had a fondness for red nail varnish and Coty's L'Aimant perfume and had a few pieces of valuable jewellery, which she wore regularly. In one of many letters, Enid wrote:

> I can't tolerate you thinking that I am materialistic. I am not as materialistic as I may appear – the things I think about, the deeper side of life I have not very much discussed with anyone, because I have met very few people who bother to think for themselves. Now you must be different because you actually chose your religion when adult, and you are serious about it – though you don't try to

force it on anyone. I would like a personal God like yours, but I find it difficult to believe in one that you can talk to as you do. I am not entirely without belief as you see. I do truly want to be as decent as I can and would like help to be, if it's possible. It is because you get it, I do want to know and I don't mind learning from you.

While she obviously wanted to understand as much as possible about Dorothy's firmly held religious beliefs, Enid did not start going to church and only joined Dorothy at Mass twice, even when she joined the family on a three-week holiday to the Isle of Wight and visited the local church several times. Enid tended to spend Sundays doing her accounts. Eventually Enid decided against a conversion to Catholicism, but it did not affect their friendship and she and Dorothy continued to meet as frequently as they could. Enid's children were extremely fond of their 'Auntie Dorothy' and they also remained close friends with her for many years. Later Imogen recalled: 'I benefited too from Dorothy's visits, as one of her "babies", from her fun and humour and insistence that no one should feel self-pity.' Imogen added that she had never known her mother to have another friend and tried to explain the surprising bond between them: 'There is no doubt that here was an attraction of opposites. My mother was creative and impulsive; Dorothy was practical and calm. My mother was beset by doubts and fears beneath her successful managing exterior; Dorothy, a Catholic convert, was secure in her faith. My mother wanted to be cherished, Dorothy was protective.'

Enid was not afraid to let Dorothy see her faults either, and revealed a rare level of self-awareness telling her:

Deep down in me I have an arrogant spirit that makes me a bit scornful of other people, if I think they are stupid or led by the nose, or at the mercy of their upbringing and environment – unable to think for themselves. I keep it under because I want to be charitable, but I have at times been horrid and contemptuous – really I have.

Before long Enid was dependent on Dorothy for all her emotional and spiritual guidance, and she made no attempt to hide the depth and strength of her feelings:

You said I was bossy – well I am – more than you think. In my mind I like to dominate even though I don't appear to be doing so. I want to hear all you have to say even if I argue at first and go all around things. You can say anything to me. I want you to. I will be willing to be taught by you because I respect you and believe in you in a way I have never felt for anyone else. I never thought for one moment that I could come to you for help like this a few months ago.

Enid mentioned Dorothy's frequent visits in her diary, and recorded how they 'talked all morning and afternoon'. She wanted to tell Dorothy everything, although she still lied about her mother and pretended she was dead. Enid had very few friends, and joining other women for social interaction or sharing confidences had never been important before. Dorothy completely changed her attitude towards women and she treasured their special friendship. In another of her lengthy and emotionally charged letters to Dorothy she gushed:

I have always wanted to be good and do good as much as lay in my power. I felt I would have to find out about you and your beliefs, not condescendingly but humbly. I told you in one of my letters that intellectual pride was the sin that really did hold me back – I thought so much of myself and my opinions and now I know I was wrong. I shall never be so high and mighty again.

The quality that Enid admired most in Dorothy was her great sense of fairness. In almost all of the stories Enid wrote after she met Dorothy being fair and loyal was considered very important and her characters were often furious when they sensed injustice. Anyone unkind or unsupportive usually got their come-uppance in the end. And although Enid herself could often be hot tempered and harsh, fairness was a trait she always demanded in others. For Dorothy's part, she was completely fascinated by Enid who may have been ruthless, ambitious and single minded, but was certainly never boring. And Dorothy was a woman who was glad to be needed. She was fond of the children who were clearly lacking in a conventional mother figure, and felt she was essential in ensuring that various domestic aspects of the Pollocks' family life ran smoothly.

It was the most significant female friendship either of them had ever known, and it has been implied that they may have actually fallen in love and had a sexual relationship. Both Imogen and Dorothy's nephew Anthony Richards who knew her very well were certain that they were not lovers: 'It has been suggested that there may have been some homosexual attraction between these two women; and that Dorothy's presence harmed my mother's first marriage and may have helped to destroy it,' Imogen wrote later. 'Dorothy was incapable of destroying relationships and too perceptive not to see if her presence was a danger.' In the children's mind Dorothy was more like a sister to Enid as she was having to come to terms with the realisation that her marriage was not the idyllic romantic fairy tale she had imagined it would be.

After Gillian and Imogen came along, Enid and Hugh had less time for each other and it became clear how little they actually had in common. Hugh was deeply depressed, not just about how little he felt wanted or needed by his wife, but also by his fear over the state of the world as Europe teetered on the brink of another world war. As a result of his political conversations with Winston Churchill, and the outbreak of the Spanish Civil War, Hugh was certain that the future was very bleak indeed. Meanwhile, Enid was gaining in confidence professionally, and he was left feeling redundant as the traditional roles of their marriage had been reversed. Enid was cheerful and self-assured when it came to her work but was feeling increasingly despondent about her husband's dark moods and became frustrated with his anti-social behaviour. In despair, Hugh would drink more to console himself, but feared that if she discovered what he was up to, Enid would have no sympathy and would resent him even more than she already seemed to. And so he would hide away in the cellar for hours and drink himself into oblivion.

The gardener Dick Hughes was the only other person who was entrusted with a key to the cellar, so that he could faithfully clear out Hugh's stack of empty bottles following his frequent bouts of heavy drinking. Nobody but Dick had any idea what Hugh was up to until he became seriously ill in 1938 and the secret stash of bottles was discovered. For a long time Enid had been unaware of what was going on in her own house, as her priority had been impressing Dorothy, and they would often leave Hugh to his own devices for long periods at a time.

When Dorothy was not visiting, Enid spent far less time with the children. Normally the girls would be allowed to go downstairs to the lounge from the nursery for just an hour each evening when Enid finished work, and she would play board games such as dominoes or snakes and ladders with them. Imogen admitted: 'I was a little wary of her but she could make the game great fun and the hour, if a little tense, was certainly a release from the boredom of the nursery.' Even when Hugh was home, he would not join the children's games, preferring to sit in his favourite chair, wearing his traditional Scottish Crawford tartan kilt. Afterwards, the nanny would give the children a bath and read them a story before putting them to bed, although Enid's own bedroom was right next door. The only other time they would be allowed to visit the lounge was to collect their sixpence pocket money each Saturday morning. Enid paid them regularly and efficiently, just as she paid the rest of her staff at the end of each week.

Despite her entire career being devoted to improving children's literacy, Enid hardly ever read to her own children. Imogen only remembers her mother reading to them once, sharing the proofs of a book she had written under the pseudonym Mary Pollock to see if she could reach the same level of success without relying on her famous name. *The Children of Kidillin* was an adventure set in Scotland at the start of the war, and she read it out loud to Gillian and Imogen first to see if they could guess that she had written it: 'She lost herself in the story just as she had when she was writing it,' Imogen said. She was delighted when the publication was successful, but when critics suggested the new author was even better than Enid Blyton, she decided to come clean and the books were reprinted under her real name.

The girls had been captivated but apart from that occasion, bedtime rituals were usually left to the nanny. Enid would take them to visit the lending library, which was to be found in their local branch of Boots the chemist, and she also made sure she was the one to take them for their regular appointments at the dentist. Having always suffered from bad teeth herself, Enid was sympathetic to the pain of the dentist's drill. Enid struggled to bond with her children and lacked entirely in maternal instincts. While she seemed to have no trouble sending warm letters to children she did not know, she seemed unable to show the same level of interest in her own flesh and blood. She was often irritated when they interrupted her work, and sometimes would not acknowledge them at all if she was busy. Imogen found both her parents cold and distant, and once said about Enid: 'There was no special relationship. There was scarcely a relationship at all.'

Although she would often mention her daughters in her writing and when talking to other adults, giving the impression she was very fold of them, the girls felt that Enid took more pride in her books than her children. Imogen wrote:

> She rarely displayed that pride and sense of wonder at these creations of hers, which so consistently did over her books and stories. My mother did not discuss other people's children a great deal. She preferred to think of them as her own friends and loyal readers, and with that compensation there was little need to worry about the less satisfactory relationship with her own children.

The girls felt starved of physical affection, and years later Imogen would recall a rare visit from Dick Hughes. She ran into his arms for a hug but she was too big for him to lift her by then and she fell back: 'That is the last occasion that I can remember either seeking or being given real physical affection as a child,' she said. Despite keeping contact to a minimum, Enid would lose her temper with the children, and beat them with a hairbrush as punishment for lying or being rude – often while their father sat nearby doing nothing. Imogen recalled: 'I yelled with pain because my mother used a hairbrush on my bare bottom, but my father did not stir. The next time I yelled for myself rather than for an audience.'

In her scathing autobiography Imogen added: 'My mother was arrogant, insecure and without a trace of maternal instinct. Her approach to life was childlike, and she could be spiteful, like a teenager.'

Chapter Eight

Despite the demands of two very young children, Enid agreed to take on even more work and began publishing *Sunny Stories* magazine every Friday from January 1937, including a weekly 'Letter from Old Thatch' which had regular updates about the girls, their domestic life and of course the antics of their pet dog Bobs – even though he had died two years earlier. Her first serial for the magazine was 'The Adventures of the Wishing Chair', and after asking children what they thought of it, Enid was swamped with hundreds of letters from readers giving their enthusiastic opinions and it was soon brought out as a book. Its phenomenal success quickly led to many, many more adventure books and Enid rushed to keep pace with the demands of her ravenous readership. Buoyed by the success of *The Wishing Chair* stories, Enid followed it up with tales about her daughter's favourite doll, *Naughty Amelia Jane*, which she and Dorothy dreamt up together when they were playing with Gillian in the nursery during one of Dorothy's many happy visits.

A rave review of *Naughty Amelia Jane* in *Teacher's World* perfectly summed up Enid's popularity: 'Another example not only of Enid Blyton's ingenuity as a story writer, but her incomparable gift of knowing just how young children like a story to be.' She had hit upon a successful formula, which changed very little from that point onwards. By the end of 1937 she had published sixteen new stories not aimed at teachers or schools, including Christmas annuals, collections of short stories, *The Green Goblin Book* and *The Yellow Fairy Book*.

Between her work, the children and her intense relationship with Dorothy, Enid had very little time left for Hugh and by the summer of 1938 they were virtually living separate lives. She was so distracted that he had been ill for several weeks before she noticed that he was having difficulty breathing and appeared to be on the verge of collapse. By the time she became sufficiently concerned to call a doctor out to the house, Hugh was suffering from a serious bout of pneumonia and was immediately admitted to hospital where his condition took a turn for the worse. Enid was shocked by how unwell her husband had become without her realising, and as his fever became more serious she feared the worst and called his brother down from Scotland. Enid was terrified that she might lose Hugh. But the fever passed after a few days and Hugh began to make a slow recovery, although it would be another month before he was well enough to return home. The crisis was enough to remind Enid how much she loved him, and could not bear the thought of life without him by her side. Of course, she told her readers all about the drama, explaining in her *Teacher's World* column: 'Gillian's Daddy has been very ill indeed and I have had to keep staying near him. Am sure you will be glad to know that he is getting better now – but it is a dreadful time when daddies or mummies are ill, isn't it?'

Hugh's illness made Enid reassess many aspects of her life, and she decided that after his convalescence, the family should not return to Old Thatch which was haunted with dark memories of his depression and alcoholism. She had initially been furious when she discovered the extent of his secret drinking binges, but over time Enid forgave his indiscretion. She felt however that the time was right for the family to make a brand new start. The house felt small with the girls growing up, and the increasing numbers of staff Enid was employing. She wanted more space but decided against building an extension as she felt it would ruin the character of Old Thatch. The house was damp and draughty and she found constantly maintaining the original thatched roof to be a worrying burden. She was also having to make increasingly frequent trips to London so she wanted to live somewhere more convenient.

Once she had made up her mind, Enid wanted to move quickly. But when Hugh discovered that Enid and Dorothy had actually chosen a new house together without consulting him, he was furious. Hugh did not like the look of the mock Tudor style property his wife had bought, and was extremely reluctant to move. The eight-bedroom house in the affluent commuter town of Beaconsfield, Buckinghamshire, was full of dark oak beams and had heavy leaded panelled windows which he thought made the place dark, gloomy and oppressive. It was set back from the road in 3 acres of grounds but the children did not like it either: 'As I grew up I came to hate its falseness,' Imogen admitted later, 'But to my mother the oak beams and the leaded panes gave her the feel of our old house in Bourne End.'

But Hugh had no say in the matter and since Imogen was just 3-years-old and Gillian was 7, they certainly were not consulted either. Hugh was not required to help with the mortgage – Enid had paid the £3,000 asking price herself with money she had earnt from writing. She was wealthy enough not to have to sell Old Thatch in order to afford the new property, so they rented it out to tenants, and Dorothy supervised whatever maintenance work needed to be done.

The new house was much more modern and less rural than Old Thatch and Hugh felt it had very little character, but there was no question that Enid would get her way in the end. Most of the arrangements for the move were already well under way while Hugh was still ill in hospital recovering from his bout of pneumonia. In order to maintain her writing commitments during the move, and to ensure she could still find time to visit Hugh regularly, Enid stayed at a guest house while the children were taken to the Isle of Wight with their nanny. As soon as Hugh was feeling strong enough to travel, Enid took him there to convalesce with the girls. They attempted to play happy families but Enid invited Dorothy to join them, and Hugh was too exhausted to play with the children or join in much of their seaside fun.

Since she was determined to plough on with the move without delay and planned to reinvent herself at the new house, Enid left behind many of their friends, and hardly bothered maintaining contact with any of them. The housekeeper Mrs Day was let go, but there was no question of Dorothy not relocating along with the rest of the family. Their relationship remained blissfully intact.

Dorothy often returned to Bourne End with Gillian and Imogen, who still preferred playing in their former garden at Old Thatch, which they missed a great deal. They had fond memories of a little well, which pumped water to the main house, and they had spent many happy hours in a Wendy house which the former gardener Dick Hughes had built for them. The children found their new home strange, empty and so cold that they slept with stone hot water bottles in their beds. They were nervous because their nursery was directly above their mother's lounge and whenever they made any noise the lamp hanging from her ceiling would rattle and infuriate her. When she heard their shrieks and screams, Enid would fly up to their room in a furious rage and slap them: 'Most of my mother's visits to the nursery were hasty, angry ones rather than benevolent,' Imogen said. She also recalled a rare visit from their former nanny Miss Herbert who made them laugh until they needed to race to the toilet, and the noise disturbed Enid while she was trying to write. Enid was incandescent at finding her daughter with her underwear around her knees, but Imogen though her mother was actually envious of the way Nanny Herbert was able to entertain the children. Imogen wrote: 'She spanked me hard and I sensed something new in her anger. It terrified me. The happy visit ended in choking tears and I added the unpleasant sensation of another person's jealousy to my collection of experiences.'

Following some renovations, the Pollock family moved in that August and Enid engaged a local employment agency to find a suitable batch of new staff to help organise the running of the house. She inherited the former owner's gardener, Mr Tapping, who tended to the sprawling lawns and fruit trees but they did not get along and she eventually dismissed him for taking vegetables, and decided she could manage the garden much more efficiently herself. However, she took on his wife Frances as her new cook. Mrs Tapping was a fierce woman who would meet with Enid in the kitchen every morning to plan the menu for the day, although before long wartime rationing would mean that meals depended very much on what was available rather than what Enid wanted. She stayed with the family for many years after her husband was killed while fighting in North Africa.

The agency also sent Mary Engler, an Austrian refugee who quickly became a favourite of Enid's. She was hired as a parlour maid but she surprised Enid with her intelligence and willingness to stand in for the nanny or cook on their days off. They became close friends and Mary confided to Enid that she had been forced to flee her home in Vienna because of the threat of war breaking out. Enid was moved by what she heard, and regularly took time away from her work to ensure that the pretty and vivacious young maid felt secure and happy. Enid even wrote to the girl's parents to reassure them that their daughter was safe, and notified the Home Office that she would take care of them all should they need to leave Austria after war was officially declared.

While the new garden was much larger, and allowed Enid to keep hens and pigeons and enough fresh flowers to fill dozens of vases, she had a rare pang of nostalgia about leaving her beloved garden at Old Thatch behind. Her usual intuition convinced her without a shadow of a doubt that her army of readers would feel exactly the same way as she did and they must be missing hearing about it too. So she decided to challenge them to come up with a name for the new house: 'I know you will be sad that Old Thatch is no longer going to be our home, because you know it so well. I am sad too because it is a beautiful place,' she wrote in *Teacher's World*. 'But I am sure you will love our new home and garden. I want you to think of a name for it.'

She gave them a detailed description of the property and its beautifully landscaped gardens, which were surrounded by high laurel hedges, and hundreds of children sent Enid their suggestions. Several weeks later she revealed that from a shortlist of finalists which included Sunny Corners, Tall Chimneys and Cherry Trees, she had eventually selected Green Hedges as it had been suggested by more readers than any other. She was so touched by the response that many of the other names appeared in her future stories and books, although Imogen felt sure her mother would have chosen Green Hedges anyway: 'I would not put it past my mother to have fiddled the statistics to enable her to choose her own name,' she said. The name became closely associated with Enid as she always put it at the top of every column from then on.

Enid may have been hoping for a fresh start for her and Hugh, but it was not to be. Hugh was miserable in the new house, and they spent even less time together as a couple than before. His health was poor too and he soon developed influenza, followed by a second severe bout of pneumonia. They also argued about global politics, with Enid convinced he was worrying about the looming global conflict unnecessarily, and she was absolutely furious at his suggestion that he would feel compelled to volunteer to join the army should he be needed. Their relationship deteriorated dramatically during this period, and he showed no sign of easing up on his drinking either.

Enid's working life continued just as frantically as it had before the move. She preferred to type outside as often as possible, and always wore something red when she wrote, since she believed the colour acted as a 'mental stimulus'. She took a short break for lunch which a maid would bring out on a tray, then worked until 5pm when she would stop to spend an hour with Gillian and Imogen, ideally in the garden, or they would be called into the lounge where she would tell them about the stories she had been writing that day. She found that they were the ideal candidates on which to test out the success of her ideas, as the stories her children liked best tended to be the ones that sold the best too. When they were older the girls were tasked with proofreading her books, and were paid a penny every time they spotted a mistake.

Enid clearly felt she was fulfilling her obligations as a mother, but the children themselves had precious few happy memories of that period. Imogen only remembered having one birthday party, given by her nanny in the nursery, since Enid did not like having their friends in the house as it broke her concentration. She did not feel the same way about Christmas, which was always a time of high excitement and Enid went to great lengths to ensure it was a truly magical day for the family. She would usually treat them all to a trip to London to see a pantomime or show at the theatre, and while she would not do any of the cooking herself, and did not go to church, Enid loved decorating the tree in secret to surprise the children, covering it in candles. She filled the house with sprigs of holly cut from the garden and paper chains which she and the girls made together. Every year she sent and received hundreds of cards, and she was inundated with gifts. Enid carefully wrapped presents for the staff, and filled stockings which Gillian and Imogen opened in bed early on Christmas morning. And when the children were old enough to buy her presents themselves she would squeal with joy no matter what they chose. Christmas was also one of the rare occasions that Enid would revisit the piano as an adult, although she had played every day as a child. Many years of never ending piano practice when she was younger had destroyed Enid's love of playing but over the festive period she delighted in entertaining the children with traditional carols, as well as some of her own tunes and some composed by her brother Hanly, whose son Carey later created the famous song 'Bananas in Pyjamas'.

Christmas Day and Boxing Day were the only occasions when the children were allowed to join their parents in the formal dining room. The rest of the time they would eat in the nursery and Enid had a quiet dinner with Hugh after they were in bed. She would then get straight back to work, usually answering letters until well into the evening, although she was strict about getting enough sleep too. She was never pleased when unexpected visitors dropped by and disrupted her rigid routine.

Enid left the running of Green Hedges entirely to her staff but the garden was very much her domain. She took great pleasure in wandering along the gravel path which ran around the lawn, tending to her pink rambler roses which grew over the pergolas. The garden also boasted a Roman sundial, bird table and a dovecote where she would leave food for fantail pigeons. Enid would take her leftover breakfast out every morning, and could recognise all the birds that visited not just from their appearance but also by their song. There was a statue of a little girl listening, a lawn for games of croquet and a large sandpit and swings for the children. There was also an area of long grass which was deliberately left untended to attract wildlife, although it seemed sinister and unwelcoming to the children who referred to it as 'Witches Lawn'. She also had an air raid shelter build when, as Hugh had predicted, the Second World War was declared in 1939. If Enid was troubled by the outbreak, she did not show it, instead she made one brief mention of it in a 'Letter from Bobs': 'Did you know we were at war with the Germans?' the dog apparently wrote. 'Well, we are. Gillian told me.' Life very much went on as usual for Enid who simply instructed her housekeeper to add blackout material to all the windows and hung gas masks in the hall.

The bomb shelter meant Gillian and Imogen were able to stay at home while many of Enid's readers living in cities were not so lucky and had to be evacuated to rural areas. Enid saw the positive side to the upheaval, and cheerfully reassured the children that it would mean they could learn about wildlife: 'Some of you have left your homes and are in the country,' she wrote. 'You will be able to see, hear, smell and enjoy all the loveliness of the countryside and you will make the most of your stay there. You are the guests of the kindly country folk and will do your best to help them.' It was a turbulent time for many children sent away from their families, but Enid wanted to reassure them that the cosy world they had left behind would still be waiting for them when they eventually returned. Gillian said later that was part of the reason Enid's books always had such cheerful settings: 'The whole ambience of the books was to remind children of what life had been like and to assure them that those times would come back again,' she explained.

But the war was not as far away as Enid liked to pretend. Even in Beaconsfield they could hear the sound of anti-aircraft bombs attacking London during the Blitz and would often watch from their windows as fighter planes made their way towards the capital at night. They watched as Allied bombers flew overhead to Germany, and even witnessed a plane crash into nearby woods. They spent one long and frightening night in the underground shelter in the garden, listening to the unknown threat overhead. Enid read the children stories and appeared to enjoy the drama, telling them it was nothing to be afraid of as it was just like a loud thunderstorm.

When food rationing was introduced, Enid's love of gardening meant they still had as much fresh produce as ever. The hens laid plenty of eggs, although if she complained in one of her columns that she was missing something she was sent food parcels – one reader even sent butter from Australia. Of course by the time the food arrived it was way past its prime and often inedible but Enid always kept the gifts she received from readers. She was also sent pet food and seeds to feed the birds in her garden, and was inundated with donations of bones for Bobs, tins of sardines for the cats and home-made treats for her own children. She even received a terrier once, when she happened to mention that one of her own dogs had gone missing. She gave her own cigarette coupons to Dorothy. In turn Enid did her bit to help the war effort by urging her readers to knit squares that could be sewn together to make blankets. By the start of 1941 she had sent over 3,000 blankets to the Red Cross, having sewed many of the squares together herself. Enid also urged children to join the 'Dig for Victory' campaign and grow their own vegetables.

Although there was a shortage of paper during the war and most authors had difficulty getting new books published, Enid lent her support to an enterprising idea to combat the rationing, turning offcuts from the popular *Picture Post* magazine into tiny 3in by 6in cartoon booklets for children. The managing editor of Brockhampton Press, E.A. Roker, had come up with the original scheme, which was a great success, and in 1942 the company had sold more than 10,000 copies of *Mary Mouse and the Dolls House*. More and more titles followed as thousands of children across the country started to collect the miniature booklets which sold for just a shilling each. And Enid cleverly signed with several new publishers in order to get the best of each one's limited paper supplies. Editors were confident that anything she wrote would sell out as soon as it was printed, and were so certain of success, that even at the times when paper rationing was at its worst, other authors saw their titles scrapped to allow extra supplies of paper for Enid's latest books. It became very difficult to obtain copies of well-established and popular titles, but there was a constant supply of Enid's books, both old and new. She was considered a very safe bet for the publishers who were only too willing to pay higher prices for whatever paper supplies they could get their hands on. And their faith in her was justified when new titles sold out almost immediately, and they would receive sacks of angry letters from disappointed readers who had been unable to buy a copy.

Despite the Blitz warnings, Enid travelled up to London for regular meetings with her publishers. Fast becoming one of the most popular authors in the country, she managed to have eleven books published in 1940 alone, including *The Secret Island*, about children who ran away from unkind relations and survived on a remote island, with *Tales of Betsy May*, *The Secret of Spiggy Holes*, *Twenty-Minute Tales* and *The Children of Cherry Tree Farm* following in quick succession. Librarians were happy to fill the shelves with her books, if only because there was so little else available as hardly any new titles for children were being published at that time. In 1941 Methuen published her retelling of Jean de Brunhoff's classic French series for children about Babar the elephant, as part of the series *Modern Classics*, which also included books by the publisher's other star authors A.A. Milne and Kenneth Grahame.

That was also the year Enid published *The O'Sullivan Twins*, which was thought to be one of the very few times she revealed the feelings of resentment she still held towards her mother over her father leaving. In the book Margery tells Lucy:

It's probably my own silly fault. You see – my mother died when I was little. And my father married again and my stepmother didn't like me. She said awful things about me to my father and he ticked me off like anything. I loved him awfully – I still do, of course, I'd give anything in the world to make him have a good opinion of me. He's so marvellous.

Regardless of her success, Enid and Hugh could not ignore the onward march of the war, nor the fact that Prime Minister Anthony Eden was publically calling on all able-bodied men to join the armed forces to help Britain's defence effort. Enid fervently hoped that Hugh's patriotic streak would not get the better of him, and he would put his health first, but like so many men across the country, Mr Pollock was determined to do whatever he could to serve his country, and was eager to get back in uniform. Enid begged him to reconsider but her protests fell on deaf ears. She felt he was being selfish, abandoning his family just as her father had done, and urged him to stay at home with her and the children. But Hugh felt a strong sense of duty and volunteered to rejoin his old regiment, the Royal Scots Fusiliers, but he was not a young man so was spared the front line. Instead he was dispatched to the Home Guard, as Commandant of the War Office School for Instructors at an army base in Dorking, Surrey. It was a decision that would ultimately destroy his second marriage.

Chapter Nine

Hugh's new role meant he was required to spend long periods away from home and it was a lonely time for Enid. It did not help matters that her loyal friend Dorothy was in great demand as a nurse and had hardly any spare time to meet with her. Petrol rationing also meant Enid was cut off from friends, and felt bereft. Enid hated the lack of adult company but after a few weeks, she realised she was actually rather relieved not to have to deal with the burden of Hugh's heavy drinking binges and his gloomy attitude, and so she decided to entertain at home for a change. It was inevitable that Enid, who had never done very well if left to her own devices, would find herself unable to resist the attentions of other men. She needed to be cared for and cherished, so when she found herself pursued, her marriage was effectively over.

She started to host regular drinks parties at Green Hedges and with a newly discovered confidence Enid was enjoying the type of social life she never had in her twenties, having got married so young to a considerably older man. Her glamorous new set of friends included Lady Peppiatt, the wife of Sir Kenneth Peppiatt, the Chief Cashier at the Bank of England. She became friendly with several young army officers who had been posted nearby, as well as a bachelor doctor who moved in next door. When Dorothy visited she tried to warn Enid that her behaviour was inappropriate and she risked a scandal but Enid was bored and carried on regardless. Before long she found herself the subject of whisperings both locally and in the gossip columns of various newspapers when it emerged that her gatherings included a number of unattached men. She was highly flirtatious and there was even a rumour that visitors once arrived at the house to find her playing tennis naked.

Hugh was furious when he came home and a member of staff told him that his wife had been entertaining men in an unsuitable way in his absence. But Enid also had her suspicions about what he had been up to after receiving an anonymous phone call with the words: 'Don't let Ida crow over you.' Several years earlier during a busier period at Newnes, Hugh had struck up a successful working relationship with the novelist Ida Crowe, when she was 21 and he was 50. At the time Ida described Hugh as 'devastatingly handsome' and when he bumped into her again during a chance meeting at the War Office he invited her to help him recruit new staff at the Dorking base. Ida leapt at the opportunity, but Enid did not hear that Ida was working as Hugh's secretary until the mystery call some weeks later. Enid had not understood the significance of the pun at the time, and tried to put it out of her mind. She had not seen her husband for several weeks, and was excited about him returning home for Christmas. She wrote in December 1941 how she and the girls were busy decorating the house in preparation for 'our Daddy's' leave. But the visit was a disaster, punctuated with explosive rows, and that would be the last time Enid ever mentioned Hugh in her writing. Hugh went back to Dorking in the New Year, and Enid continued to be consoled by various admirers who seemed to provide her with precisely the companionship she required as the war raged on.

Enid knew there was speculation about her private life, and pretended not to mind. However, it must have rattled her slightly as she found herself confiding in Dorothy, and invited her to stay at Green Hedges as a chaperone, to make her living arrangements seem more appropriate. Dorothy arrived to find Enid with a man who she felt was only after her money, but she was having far too much fun to listen to her friend's stern warnings. The next time Hugh returned to Green Hedges, there were yet more arguments. Given that Hugh's first marriage had broken down while he was away in similar circumstances during the First World War, he demanded to know what Enid was thinking of. She in turn confronted him about the affair with Ida Crowe. They argued constantly and it looked increasingly likely that divorce was on the cards.

Enid may have been desperately lonely, but her children were miserable too and she appeared not to notice. With Hugh away doing his bit for the war effort, Enid had a lot on her plate and hired yet another new nanny for the children. Sarah Aynsley, a young girl from Northumberland, was meant to stay only temporarily as she was due to join her fiancé in South Africa where he was working as a Methodist minister, but restrictions on almost all foreign travel meant that she ended up with the family for four years, and fell in love with a German prisoner of war who was working on a local farm. She was strict with the girls and would make them sit at the table for hours until they finished their meals, but Imogen shared a bed with her and felt a closer bond with Sarah than she ever did with Enid, and later described her as 'the most permanent close relationship of my childhood'. Imogen was particularly distraught when Sarah left, and she was sent to a small day school near Green Hedges, called High March. Imogen was left-handed, which made her rather clumsy and she had trouble with her handwriting and sewing. Although Enid had learnt how to help left-handers adapt during her Froebel teacher training, she very much tended to stay away from her children's academic progress, and was far too busy to get involved in school life, although she would reprimand the girls if they came home with poor reports at the end of term.

The girls found social interaction challenging since Enid did not encourage them to invite other children home. While Gillian did have one or two local friends, Imogen was so desperately lonely that she invented an imaginary twin called Jimmy to keep her company as she walked to and from school by herself. Although they were rarely allowed guests over to the house, many other children would simply turn up uninvited to ask Enid for her autograph or to give her presents. The war meant fewer visitors but at other times they would ring the doorbell and ask if Enid was in. According to Imogen: 'These visitors were much more welcome than friends of mine would have been.' Enid would always come and see the children at the door, and if she could spare the time she would also invite the lucky ones in to the lounge for a chat about her stories which they loved so much. She held competitions for children to win the chance to join her at home for tea parties. But while she delighted in treating them to delicious jellies and cakes, her own children were banished to the nursery. These tea parties were as much for Enid's benefit as the fans, as she could really allow herself to be one of the kids. Gillian and Imogen found it confusing when other children visited Green Hedges since they almost never saw this warm and amiable side to their mother. She obviously found it far easier to relate to unknown children, whom she saw as friends, than to her own offspring who expected so much more: 'My mother's love of children was real enough,' Imogen wrote years later. 'It was only her own children and those belonging to her staff or close friends who somehow failed to capture her love. Her feelings were of friendship, of intense loyalty and of sharing. They were not maternal at all.'

Enid's own daughters were routinely wheeled out to pose for happy family portraits and interviews where she talked cheerfully about the delicate balancing act she performed between her punishing self-imposed deadlines and her role as a devoted mother. But they scarcely recognised the woman she described. Enid wanted to seem as if she lived in the blissful, carefree life she described on paper, full of crumpets for tea and idyllic picnics – washed down with lashings of ginger beer – but the reality was vastly different, and the children soon felt she was coldly exploiting them to further promote the Blyton brand.

As well as keeping her daughters at arm's length, Enid had grown even further away from Hugh as well. Being forced to spend increasing amounts of time apart when their marriage was already so rocky proved disastrous for Mr and Mrs Pollock. Her working relationship with Newnes was lessening as she signed lucrative contracts with various other publishers, and entertaining unsuitable men behind her husband's back was not the only risk Enid took that year. She also wrote a frightening book for the first time. *The Secret Mountain*, which focused on children searching for adults who had been lost in a plane crash, shocked and disturbed young readers. Peggy, Mike and Nora's parents disappeared on a flight to Australia, leaving them in the care of a cold-hearted uncle and aunt. A local boy named Jack helped them escape to the island, and ended up becoming the leader of their group as he could catch rabbits and fish, and knew which nuts and berries to gather for them to eat. Together they created a paradise-like hideaway, and managed to survive against the odds, even tackling the onset of winter until they were reunited with their parents just in time for Christmas. Enid admitted she was inspired by reading *Robinson Crusoe* as a child and at one point the character Peggy said: 'It will be fun to read about Robinson Crusoe because he was alone on an island, just as we are. I guess we could teach him a few things though!' Her publishers feared she had staked her reputation with this major new departure, but Enid accurately predicted that her readers were far too loyal to desert her over one minor blip.

A few months after Hugh's fateful Christmas visit home, in the spring of 1941, Dorothy persuaded Enid to join her on a trip to visit her sister Betty Marsh at her home near Budleigh Salterton in Devon. Enid was reluctant at first, claiming she was too busy to make the long journey, but hoped a change of scene would help her clear her head and work out a way to patch things up with Hugh. But that trip sealed their fate as Dorothy unwittingly introduced Enid to the man who would destroy her marriage.

In Devon the ladies were joined by some of Betty's friends from London who also happened to be staying in the area on a golfing holiday. Among them was a handsome surgeon called Kenneth Fraser Darrell Williams, and from the first moment he and Enid met over a game of bridge one evening, she suddenly no longer had the slightest flicker of interest in attempting any kind of a reconciliation with Hugh. It was love at first sight for both of them, the chemistry between Enid and Kenneth was instant and overwhelming. He was captivated by her quick wit and their lively conversation from that very first evening, and she was enormously flattered by holding the attention of such a handsome doctor. They talked for hours, both confiding that their marriages were unhappy and revealed that they argued with their spouses. Enid even told Kenneth how hurt she had been by her father leaving when she was a child.

Kenneth was an athletic man with thick, dark hair who had excelled at Oxford University after winning a scholarship and went on to gain a first class degree from Keble College. He served as a surgeon with the Royal Navy in the First World War but his ship was torpedoed in the Battle of Jutland and the resulting explosion blew out both his eardrums. Returning home he served with the Royal Air Force as a doctor on the ground, before completing his medical training at St Bart's Hospital in London. He had been promised a job at the eminent hospital, but following his shocking experiences on the battlefield, Kenneth was a very different person when he returned. He had witnessed the deaths of many of his friends, and was one of very few young men from his year at Oxford who survived the war.

His severe deafness left him feeling shy, isolated and increasingly bitter. Although he rarely had much trouble hearing Enid when she spoke to him, Kenneth was difficult to work with and was soon asked to leave St Bart's. He landed a new position at St Stephen's Hospital in Fulham and worked his way up the ladder to a senior role. Just like Enid, he boasted an impressive photographic memory and went on to have a glittering career in the medical profession. He was highly regarded by other surgeons and gambled successfully on horse racing and the stock market.

The pair were so drawn to each other that they spent every day together for the rest of the holiday, and as soon as they returned home embarked on an illicit affair and made every effort to meet as often as possible. Kenneth was also married, but had no children and assured a besotted Enid that it was over between him and his wife. They met as often as they could in secret, and it is believed that it was Kenneth who destroyed many key pages of Enid's diaries from this turbulent period in her private life. Enid rented a discreet flat in London, using Dorothy's name to avoid any unwanted attention since any story about her made great fodder for the newspapers. The strong moral and ethical code which was deemed so very important for characters in her stories was certainly not something Enid adhered to in her private life.

As often as they could get away, Enid and Kenneth would rush to their love nest for romantic liaisons. They were devoted to each other.

While Hugh was still based at the army training camp in Dorking, Kenneth also started to visit her at Green Hedges and was introduced to the children in early 1942. He even removed Imogen's tonsils at home after they became infected, and bombing meant staying in hospital would be too dangerous for her. Kenneth summoned an anaesthetist he knew from London and performed the operation on the scullery table. Doubtless Enid was frantic with worry, but Kenneth calmly took control of the situation and she was relieved that for the first time in a long while she did not have to be the strong one. It strengthened their bond and from then on Kenneth would not allow any other doctor to operate on the family. He nursed Gillian when she suffered concussion after being knocked unconscious by a lorry while cycling in the road, and removed her appendix when she was 16. On another occasion he was on hand to nurse Enid's wounds when she was attacked by a dog while playing golf.

'Uncle' Kenneth also joined Enid and the girls on a two-week family holiday to the exclusive Grosvenor Hotel in Swanage that summer, with Dorothy acting as chaperone. But as far as they were aware, Kenneth was nothing more than a friend of their mother's. Although he was not used to small children, he made a great effort to get along with Gillian and Imogen. Unlike their father, he was strong and would spend hours in the garden with them playing robust physical games – giving them piggybacks and wheelbarrow races. They quickly grew fond of Kenneth although it took some time to adapt to his profound deafness. He used an old fashioned ear trumpet and could only hear voices if the speaker was facing him and enunciating very clearly. A long running history of stomach ulcers meant Kenneth was not meant to drink alcohol, so Enid cut down on her drinking too – apart from an occasional glass of stout at lunchtime to help with her anaemia. The girls did not mind him spending so much time at the house, although Enid did not tell them the true nature of their relationship and they believed for many months that it was simply platonic.

Kenneth's furious wife once made a trip to Green Hedges to confront Enid, and to accuse her of stealing her husband. She had found out about the secret love nest in Knightsbridge, but Enid, thinking quickly, completely denied cheating and said that it was in fact Dorothy who he was having the affair with. The excuse seemed plausible since the flat was rented in Dorothy's name. Dorothy was mortified, but said nothing out of loyalty to Enid and to ensure she did not suffer any bad publicity. Enid urged Dorothy not to tell the children either, because she did not want to set a bad example to them. Imogen revealed later: 'For a whole year she carried on her lives with two different men, deceiving, or appearing to deceive, everyone who might have seriously criticised her. However when lying to others she invariably lied to herself first.'

It may not have occurred to the children to doubt their mother's motives, but Hugh was highly suspicious. When he next returned from Dorking, he found Kenneth staying there. Kenneth attempted to cover his tracks by claiming he merely wanted to ask Hugh's advice on joining the Home Guard. But Enid had moved all his clothes and belongings into the spare bedroom, and he realised the real reason that his wife had been staying in London so often. Enid could see no other solution but ending the marriage since her heart already lay elsewhere. Hugh was humiliated; divorce was all they had left to discuss. After one last bitter argument, Hugh left home for good. Gillian walked him to Beaconsfield train station where there was a tearful farewell but she did not realise he was never coming back. Since many fathers were away in the army at that time, Enid was able to conceal the truth from the children for more than eighteen months. For a long time they had no idea that their father would not return as Enid never gave them a proper explanation, convinced they were too young to understand. She concealed the truth just as she herself had been forced to do by her own mother many years earlier when her father left.

Since Enid had already discovered that Hugh was having an affair with Ida, she insisted that she should be the one to launch the divorce petition against him to avoid any adverse publicity. She could not bear the idea that she would be thought of as an adulterer. Enid was held in high esteem as a role model and moral guardian for young people, so any stain on her character would be very bad for business. Hugh reluctantly agreed to take all the blame on the condition there would be no battle over the children, and that they would always share equal custody. He portrayed himself as the guilty party on the understanding that he would be allowed to see his daughters whenever he wanted. But Hugh never saw his children again.

Enid had changed her mind about giving him any access at all and became increasingly vindictive and blocked every attempt he made to visit. She even warned staff at the girls' school not to allow Hugh to see them, and kept his letters from them. Very quickly and with a chilling indifference Enid simply erased Hugh from all of their lives, she scrubbed out all trace of him, almost as if he had never been there. She even asked Newnes to sack him, threatening to take all her future books to rival publisher if they refused. As the company's most profitable author, Enid was their priority and they had no choice. Ida Crowe later said that Enid was determined to stop him finding any work in the publishing industry and he was eventually declared bankrupt before sinking back into depression once more.

The daughter he went on to have with Ida, Rosemary Pollock, said:

> My father was an honourable man – not the flawed inconsequential one which was the deliberate misconception perpetuated by Enid. This agreement was a sham because Enid had no intention of allowing him any kind of contact with either of the girls. She even told the girls' boarding school that on no account was their father, who was paying the bills, to be allowed near them. Gillian said the last time she saw her father was when they were walking to Beaconsfield station and she had this awful feeling she was not going to see him again. She said that on her wedding day, she looked around the church and hoped her father would turn up. My father said he was devastated not to have been invited to Gillian's wedding.

Rosemary also accused Enid of wrecking Hugh's career:

> Enid was capable of many vindictive things and she didn't want her former husband occupying a prominent position in London publishing, a world she dominated. My father had to file for bankruptcy in 1950 because he couldn't find work. She also put out a story that he was a drunk and an adulterer, and that he had made her life a misery. Incredibly, Enid even wrote to my mother three years after they had both remarried, saying: 'I hope he doesn't ruin your life as he did mine'. My father did drink, but it was in order to numb the pain. I never heard him criticise Enid. He would praise her remarkable talents.

Enid's friend Mary Engler stayed in contact with Hugh for a while, and would meet him to pass on news of the girls, but Hugh was banished from Green Hedges, and soon after Enid informed Gillian that she was being sent away to boarding school at Godstowe Preparatory School in nearby High Wycombe. Gillian assumed Enid wanted her out of the way so she could spend more time with Kenneth, and wrote later:

> There was no discussion about it and no reason was given to me. It was a shock as I was happy and doing well at school with another year to go. Looking back, I think that it was at this time my mother

and stepfather entered into a serious relationship and he was probably a far more frequent visitor once I was away from home.

Kenneth also agreed to be named as the guilty party in his own divorce on the strict understanding that Enid would not be named in any legal proceedings. She was so desperate to ensure that she was not publicly associated with the breakdown of his marriage that they actually persuaded another woman to spend a night in a hotel room with Kenneth so that he could be caught cheating, and no blame could be cast on Enid. Enid only revealed the full picture to the children once her divorce was finalised in June 1943, by which time the man they had known as simply Uncle Kenneth was also single. It emerged that they had hastily arranged a low-key wedding for 20 October 1943 at the City of Westminster Register Office. Imogen later recalled being summoned to her mother's bedroom where Enid broke the unexpected news in her typically blunt fashion: 'She said that my father, my first father would never come back. I burst into tears of surprise and shock at this news and cried, I think, not because I loved my father, but for opportunities lost and second chances wiped out; much as one may after a death. My mother was shocked.'

But, according to Imogen, Enid dealt with her daughter's tears briskly, and after just 5 minutes she was dismissed from the bedroom. Gillian meanwhile was informed by staff at her boarding school. The girls were confused when Enid suggested they forget all about Hugh, and that an exciting future was in store for them all. They did not attend the wedding and immediately afterwards, without consulting them, Enid changed all their surnames to Darrell Waters in a further bid to help preserve her wholesome public image. She told the girls it was 'So we can all be one family.' Enid knew she and Kenneth could not stay together any longer without being married for the sake of her reputation, as her divorce had already made headline news and it certainly would not have been appropriate for her to live with another man. She had not forgotten the whispered accusations about her private life when Hugh was away, and she was eager to repair the damage and present herself to the public as a wholesome and devoted wife once again. Kenneth may have been a divorcee himself, but at least he was a respectable surgeon.

Six days after Enid's second wedding, Hugh married Ida Crowe, who went on to give Enid a run for her money in the publishing world by producing 123 romantic novels in a prolific career which ended up spanning 9 decades – Ida was still writing when she died at the age of 105 in 2013. Many of her dashing male heroes, whom she said were based on Hugh, tended to be rugged older war veterans who rescued breathless naïve virgins from danger in novels with risqué titles such as *White Heat* and *Interlude for Love*. Ida explained: 'I never got bored of it because it's something I absolutely love. My books are full of hope and romance rather than sex.'

And like Enid, Ida worked astonishingly fast, at one point producing forty books in five years, and claimed she could finish a novel in just six weeks. She used ten pseudonyms and saw seventy of her steamy tales published by Mills & Boon under names including Pamela Kent, Rose Burghley, Susan Barrie and Mary Whistler. When she became unable to use a typewriter, Ida dictated her steamy stories to Rosemary, the daughter she had with Hugh, at their home near Looe in Cornwall. Speaking shortly before she died, Ida explained the secret of her own enduring success:

> A romance is never just a romance, there's adventure, mystery and movement. You need a grand, dramatic setting – the Swiss Alps were always a personal favourite of mine – and a chance meeting, on a train, a cruise, or perhaps the hero and heroine find themselves shipwrecked on a desert island. The men are normally rich, well-to-do – but never vulgar with their money. Young men lack the maturity to take control so an older man is essential to provide the reassurance the heroine's needs. There's always a fair amount of turbulence before he sweeps in to save the day. A happy ending is an absolute must.

When Ida and Hugh were first married and Enid had ensured he was sacked, money was tight and he had been left with little option but to take a job he was offered in America, advising on civil defence matters. Gillian and Imogen heard so little of their father from then on that they were stunned to be introduced to their 'brother' years later at a family wedding. They had no idea that Hugh had another child, a boy called Alistair from his first marriage, but they had little in common and lost touch. The next time they heard of their father was when Hugh phoned Green Hedges, having heard that Gillian was getting married. Imogen recognised his distinctive Scottish accent immediately but panicked at the thought of what her mother might think, and lied to Hugh, claiming she was a secretary. The girls grew up with very few strong memories of their natural father.

Once she became Mrs Darrell Waters, Enid successfully reinvented herself once again.

Chapter Ten

It soon felt as if Hugh had never actually lived at Green Hedges at all, as it quickly became Kenneth's home. He was certainly there far more often than Hugh had ever been, he returned from work promptly each evening, unless a bomb blast in London meant all the doctors at St Stephen's Hospital in Chelsea had to work longer hours to treat extra patients. But Enid never complained; she stopped work as soon as he came home, and they spent every weekend together. The spare bedroom where Hugh had slept became Kenneth's dressing room. Kenneth was 51-years-old by the time they married, and had no children of his own, so their first Christmas together as a family in 1943 was a joyous occasion since he loved the festivities nearly as much as Enid. He arranged party games for them all to play together, in a way Hugh had never done, and Imogen later recalled: 'My stepfather hated to lose, but he could often praise the winner and those evening hours in the holidays were among the best of family times.'

Kenneth learnt to control his violent temper, but he could still be prone to aggressive outbursts aimed at the children when he thought he had Enid's best interests at heart. Imogen recalled one particularly severe reprimand from Kenneth:

He said that I was wicked and ungrateful and a terrible nuisance to my mother. If the words were cruel, the anger that exploded from him was terrifying. As I lay in bed after my stepfather had gone back downstairs, no doubt to tell my mother that he had done a good job, I slowly and grimly came to terms with the fact that I would never again be able to talk about myself, my worries, problems and joys. I began to build a wall around my inner self so that I could never be hurt in that way again.

Imogen never forgot that night which marked her for the rest of her life. In her autobiography she went on: 'My mother, a woman indeed now but not in any emotional sense a mother, was I am sure completely unaware of what she had done when she sent my stepfather up to deal with me. It had been an irritating event indeed, but not one to dwell on, for as a person she was busy and fulfilled.'

Although Gillian had a few fond memories from returning to Green Hedges in the school holidays throughout her teens, Imogen started to feel very isolated. She wrote:

> I believed that my mother did not really like me and indeed, I did not like her much either. Perhaps we saw in each other things of ourselves that we could not accept. Her relationship with my sister was much easier. My stepfather continued to accept us both with goodwill, but I had closed myself against any friendship with him for fear of his anger.

Imogen had joined her sister at Godstowe, and although it was only 6 miles away, Enid rarely visited, except when Imogen's behaviour got so bad that she was threatened with expulsion. Imogen recalled the day her mother came into her own after hearing that her daughter had been rude and broken beds by bouncing on them: 'She descended upon the school and told our housemistress that she had never heard anything so ridiculous as expelling a girl for such minor misdemeanours, and that she simply would not accept it.' She feared that any bad behaviour at school could damage her public image as a positive role model for children. Imogen recalled: 'At the beginning of every holidays, my mother would summon me and would tell me how ashamed she was, and once, justifiably perhaps because I had almost been expelled, that I was harming her reputation.'

Enid's outburst did the trick, and Imogen was allowed to stay, but the war meant there was a high turnover of staff at the school, leaving the children unstable and confused. Imogen felt she had been packed off to boarding school to relieve her mother of the burden of responsibility so she and Kenneth could be free to start their married life unencumbered. Kenneth was Enid's priority now. Imogen recalled: 'Bit by bit her life was taking the shape it needed and the awkward past was being put behind her.'

And while Enid and Kenneth were clearly besotted with one another, they were both as stubborn as each other too, and they would bicker from the start. However, he learnt to tolerate her temper, and made allowances for the pressure she put herself under when she was working. The household staff also knew to keep quiet when Enid was busy and generally life at Green Hedges was peaceful.

Despite his profound deafness, which worsened as he got older meaning he could rarely be without his ear trumpet, Kenneth remained active and full of enthusiasm for various sporting activities, and shared Enid's passion for gardening and the outdoors. They also shared a similar childish sense of humour and enjoyed the same type of jokes and love of card games, especially bridge. Luckily Enid had learnt to speak very clearly when she was a teacher, so Kenneth could always understand her. She found their long conversations particularly helpful when she was developing a new plot, and had trouble sleeping. Enid would make him laugh with her impersonations, and the couple were very proud of each other's professional successes.

Kenneth was a regular churchgoer, and would encourage the girls to join him at Sunday services at the Church of St Michael and All the Angels at Beaconsfield. But Enid never attended church until Gillian got married. She had lost her faith when her father died, and besides exploring Catholicism with Dorothy and retelling Old Testament stories in one of her early books, *Tales from the Bible*, she very rarely mentioned religion. In one later story, *House at the Corner*, a rebellious teenage girl called Pam sneaked into a church service and was surprised to find it calming and comforting: 'It was a good place to come in when you were in trouble,' she thought to herself.

Enid and Kenneth did not have a large circle of acquaintances, but struck up a close friendship with new neighbours, Gordon and Ida Biggs who moved in to Upton Leigh, the house next door with their four children, Diana, Keith, Jennifer and Elizabeth. The children, who made a gap in the hedge so they could run between the two houses, were rather star struck by their famous neighbour. Elizabeth said: 'She was incredibly vibrant, an absolutely vital person. Everyone else in the room sort of faded. It was just this incredible personality sitting on the settee.'

The cost of her second marriage was that Enid had to sacrifice her intimate relationship with Dorothy. She had been upset by Enid's decision to remarry so soon after her divorce, and refused to attend the wedding. And a few months later, in the summer of 1944, Enid destroyed the remaining shreds of their friendship entirely. Dorothy was resentful of Kenneth, but an emergency left her with no choice but to call Enid begging for her help; her family had been bombed out of their house in Twickenham and Dorothy was desperate for a place to stay with her sister Betty, nephew Anthony Richards and her boss Freddy Chambers. They asked for shelter and of course Enid agreed at once that they must all come and stay at Green Hedges. But if Dorothy had been hoping for sympathy as well as a practical solution from her closest friend, she was bitterly disappointed. Enid said she wanted to help, but within two days of their arrival it was evident that Enid was extremely annoyed by the upheaval of having so many visitors in the house. Anthony later recalled being deeply stung after hearing Enid say: 'That boy will never face up to life.'

Of course her staff took care of all the necessary domestic arrangements but Enid complained about the extra burden in her *Teacher's World* column, blaming the visitors for not leaving her time to answer her letters: 'I have had such a busy week,' she wrote. 'Five people who had been bombed out of their house suddenly came to me with their kitten, so, as you can imagine, I have not had much time to do anything beyond getting beds for them and looking after them.' Dorothy, who had never asked Enid for help before, was utterly mortified at the cold way she and her family were treated in their hour of need. Dorothy was used to Enid's unpredictable moods, but matters were made even worse when 'Letters from Bobs' appeared, with the dog apparently complaining too: 'We have had a houseful of people this week and everywhere I went I bumped into somebody.' Despite the embarrassment, Enid refused to apologise for her behaviour, and Dorothy was so furious that the pair did not speak again for ten years. The girls missed her a great deal but Enid was very good at dismissing anything unpleasant from her mind and not explaining it at all if she did not want to. For many years she and Dorothy had been devoted to one another, but once Enid met Kenneth she no longer needed her. Enid was only capable of one intimate relationship at a time.

Kenneth accepted whatever reason Enid gave him for Dorothy's family's sudden departure, as he would always take her side in any argument. After peace was declared across Europe and life began to settle back to normal Enid found a new best friend, a new parlour maid named Doris Cox. Doris was a bright, red-haired woman who had served with the Women's Auxiliary Air Force during the war, and admitted she had never heard of Enid Blyton when she was sent from the employment agency in High Wycombe. Doris who had no relatives of her own, slotted cheerfully into life at Green Hedges and became so devoted to the family that she stayed by Enid's side until she died, nursing her every day until the very end. She shared Enid's great love of wildlife, and was one of very few people able to distract her when she was working to come out into the garden to see an unusual bird or insect. Doris' cousin George Cox was a keen gardener too, and Enid put him in charge of landscaping whenever she felt like changing the look of the grounds.

Enid entered into a phase of contentment with Kenneth. Imogen described her at the time: 'As a middle aged woman she radiated a cheerful confidence which successfully masked any remaining insecurities.' And while it may have been a time of economic austerity across Britain, that was certainly not the case for the Darrell Waters who had become very wealthy indeed. They opened a joint bank account and while Enid was still cautious when it came to spending, Kenneth liked treating his wife to the finer things in life. He became a regular customer at Biggs of Maidenhead, an expensive jewellery shop where he would select pieces of modern diamond jewellery for Enid. He also enjoyed buying her fur coats and commissioned a portrait of her by the artist Aubrey Claude Davidson-Houston, in which she wore a string of pearls and a diamond brooch he had bought for her – with her own money of course. But while he enjoyed splashing their money around, he was oddly careful in areas where tiny amounts could be saved, and would deliver letters by hand whenever possible to save the cost of a stamp, and if the letter contained a paperclip he would even wait for people to open the envelope so he could bring it back. If there was a delay connecting his telephone calls Kenneth would be known to march down to the exchange in person and demand an explanation.

Fiercely protective of his wife, Kenneth would also fire off legal complaints to the press, or indeed anyone who dared criticise or even publicly joke about Enid. He waged war on the BBC's constant refusal to broadcast her work on the radio. Enid could never understand why her repeated requests were always turned down. She had been sending the BBC material since 1936 but was consistently rejected and it only emerged much later that there was in fact a ban on all dramatisations of her work. Broadcasting executives considered the stories 'second rate' and lacking in literary value, according to internal messages. One note about a short story said: 'Not strong enough. It really is odd to think that this woman is a best seller. It is all such very small beer.' Another memo from Jean Sutcliffe, head of the BBC schools department, said: 'My impression of her stories is that they might do for Children's Hour but certainly not for Schools Dept, they haven't much literary value. There is rather a lot of the Pinky-winky-Doodle-doodle Dum-dumm type of name – and lots of pixies – in the original tales.' In another she wrote that she was concerned the BBC would become 'Just another victim of the amazing advertising campaign which has raised this competent and tenacious second-rater to such astronomical heights of success.' In 1940 *Children's Hour* rejected Enid's play called *The Monkey and the Barrel Organ*, on the grounds that it was 'stilted and long winded'. Enid was livid when she found out about the ban and wrote to a producer complaining: 'I and my stories are completely banned by the BBC as far as children are concerned – not

one story has ever been broadcast, and so it is said, not one ever will be.'
Although the ban was lifted in the 1950s, after almost thirty years, and she
eventually appeared on *Woman's Hour* in 1963, the critical rumblings never
really went away.

Luckily Kenneth was fully supportive of his wife, and always interested
to know what was keeping her so busy, so she would share extracts of new
stories with him. Although he was not supposed to drink, he was so proud of
her achievements that he insisted on starting a new tradition of celebrating
by opening a bottle of expensive champagne every time Enid finished a book
– no matter that by then she was producing new titles at an astonishing rate
of around twenty a year – as well as all her regular columns and features. As
the printing presses returned to full strength after the war and with paper
supplies once again able to meet the great demand from readers, Enid had
no qualms about asking her publishers for a hefty increase in royalties, from
10 to 15 per cent. She also insisted it be written into her contract that the
publishers must guarantee that each first print run be of at least 25,000 copies.
She knew she could wield great power in the industry and always got her
way. Enid chose to deal directly with her publishers, rather than via an
agent or manager, and her boss Paul Hodder-Williams, who had recently
returned from the battlefields, was impressed with Enid's commanding
attitude. He liked the way she always stuck to deadlines, was meticulous
about proofreading and spotting mistakes and was always as pleasant in
correspondence as she was at face-to-face meetings. Most people, especially
men, who encountered Enid in a professional capacity, tended to like her
and commented on how agreeable and easy she was to work with. Enid had
contracts running with over twenty different publishing houses, mostly in
the UK but also several abroad, and even she was starting to struggle with all
the various aspects of editing, marketing and distributing books herself. She
still had her say when it came to production however, insisted on choosing
the illustrators herself, and always ensured plenty of pictures, wide spacing
and clear print to make them attractive to children. Whether she was right or
wrong on these matters, it was extremely rare for anyone to dare to disagree
with their most profitable author. And over time it became hard to argue
since Enid was usually proved to be correct.

She need not have been so insistent, since most publishers knew that a
new Enid Blyton title meant a boost in profits, so would usually set aside
enough paper to produce 150,000 copies at a time as often as they could.
Throughout the 1940s and 1950s Enid wrote dozens of stories for children,
usually focused around adventure, magic, circuses or farms. She had several

different fictional stories on the go at any one time, but somehow managed to keep all the characters straight in her head. And she sent dozens of letters a week but never kept copies, relying on her excellent photographic memory should she ever be required to refer back to them. It was the most prolific period of Enid's career. As soon as the war was over, Enid felt she owed it to her loyal readers to satisfy their seemingly insatiable appetite for more stories, and in 1945 she finally gave up the column she had written for *Teacher's World* every week for almost twenty-three years. She had already been considering leaving and when she heard that the editor she had worked with since her first column was planning to retire, her mind was made up. Enid did not like change, and did not want to stick around to see what fresh ideas the new editor might have in mind for the magazine. In her final 'Letter from Green Hedges', published in November 1945, she wrote:

We have been very good friends and we always shall be. Although I shall not be writing to you any more, you know I shall be writing for you! You can always write to me if you want to. Go on doing all the things we have done together, won't you, work hard, be kind and just, be my friend as much as ever. I shall be here at Green Hedges just the same, with my children, my pets and my garden – writing books for you all as hard as ever I can.

Chapter Eleven

Enid was highly astute when it came to the children's literature market, and was keenly aware of the competition. She had noticed how popular Arthur Ransom's adventure story *Swallows and Amazons* had been when it was first published in 1930. Children could identify with his small-scale, plausible adventures set within the window of the Walker family's holiday to the Lake District. He made something unique appear quite ordinary and certainly achievable. Enid tapped into that same longing in children, and hit upon the idea for *The Famous Five* series. She already knew, through her success with weekly magazines and monthly columns, that children enjoyed the anticipation of sequels to stories being presented in regular instalments. Such was their hunger for updates about the gang that they did not seem to care that the key characters never developed or matured.

Each of the twenty-one stories in the series followed a predictable but winning formula of a holiday adventure. Julian, Dick and Anne would meet their cousin George and her dog Timmy at a country village, a rural train station or seaside resort where they would soon find themselves involved in the detection of a local crime, a treasure hunt or a baffling mystery that only they could solve. Usually their Uncle Quentin and Aunt Fanny were far too busy to take much notice of what they were up to, and most other adults were viewed with suspicion. The stories always ended happily, and wrongdoers who were powerless in the face of the gang's luck, sleuthing and eavesdropping skills would be punished accordingly.

Anne was always made to do the domestic chores – although that rarely amounted to more than opening cans of peaches or folding away the sleeping bags nicely. But many of Enid's female characters were timid, could not row, climb or swim very well, and were usually the ones to blurt out secrets. In *Five Go Off in a Caravan*, Anne was told: 'Well you're only a girl.' In *Five Get Into Trouble* Anne was stuck up a tree but unable to do anything about it:

Anne was sitting absolutely petrified up in the tree. She couldn't move or speak. She tried to call out to poor Dick but her tongue wouldn't say a word. She had to sit there and hear her brother being dragged away by two strange ruffians. She began to cry. She didn't dare to climb down because she was trembling so much she was afraid she would lose her hold and fall.

The other recurring female character Aunt Fanny had a traditional domestic role in the home, while Uncle Quentin, a brilliant scientist, was always buried in his complicated research papers. His bad tempers were forgiven because he was so busy working.

Enid was delighted with the now iconic cover illustrations by Mary Gernat, whose drawings were inspired by her four sons, Roger, Francis, Nicholas and Justin. The artist would often interrupt her children's own holiday escapades in sand dunes and rock pools to make them pose so she could quickly draw rough outlines as they played. The basic templates were later fleshed out into the colourful drawings that still adorn many of Enid's book covers today. Mary's second son Roger How later revealed how their mother would promise them extra pocket money if they modelled for her, usually along with their small brown pet dog Patch, who inspired the drawings of Timmy. Their home on the Hampshire coast proved an idyllic backdrop too. Roger explained the family's role:

> We were the perfect age to be her subjects. I was about four or five and my older brother Francis must have been about nine. She would ask us to pose like we were pulling on a rope, or firing a bow and arrow. We weren't given a rope or a bow, we just had to go through the actions, pretending. She worked very quickly so we never had to pose for long and she would give us a penny or a halfpenny as pocket money. My mother was a natural artist. She would draw a few quick lines in a couple of minutes and that was all she needed to work from. At the time we were just kids and didn't realise the importance of what she was doing. But none of the children on the finished book covers look like us, we were just recreating the poses she wanted.

Roger's father Michael also appeared as the blue pirate in a series of reading aids Enid wrote for primary schools. An unseen archive of Mary's sketches came to light many years later when a customer visiting Roger's picture-framing workshop in Hampshire commented on a box of paperback books brimming with the original drawings. Enid also developed a close working relationship with the illustrator Eileen Soper who drew pictures for many books over more than two decades, since she trusted the artist implicitly to understand what she wanted. Enid was not a woman prone to effusive praise, but she prided herself on being fair and giving credit where she felt it was due. When one of her publishers suggested that Eileen prepare some rough sketches for Enid to approve, she gave them short shrift, replying: 'I don't need to see roughs of any of her sketches. She and I have worked together for so long now and I have always found her accurate and most dependable – in fact excellent in every way.'

Incredulous adults have called *The Famous Five* books repetitive, banal and even boring, laced with racism, sexism and snobbery. But they were intended for children who found them exciting and amusing. Children did not care if the geographical locations were nonsense, or journey times were improbable or the chief characters lead impressive but totally unrealistic lifestyles – for example, George had her own island and their friend Tinker was very proud of his lighthouse. Enid knew a hit when she saw one, and she supplied new stories almost as quickly as her readers demanded. They were all much loved but her name is synonymous with *The Famous Five* books, which still remain her most popular creations with millions of children and adults alike.

Enid's experience of teaching children of various ages in one classroom at Southernhay had taught her that all children, regardless of their age, particularly enjoyed following a series. They liked getting to know the characters in greater depth through new stories. Building on popular characters which developed with each new story ensured readers were hooked, particularly in the cases of *The Famous Five*, *The Secret Seven* and the *Mystery* books. It meant that she could constantly return to her stories, tweaking, refreshing and updating them as often as she liked. They translated successfully too, her largest overseas markets being Germany and France, where more than a million copies of *The Famous Five* were sold within the first two years of publication. They were reprinted endlessly in both hardback and paperback, and four of the stories were made into films, produced on location in Enid's beloved Dorset, while a hit stage play ran in London's West End for two Christmas seasons.

The familiarity of the characters, settings and themes was something children craved. Their demands were insatiable. Enid had initially only intended to write six *Famous Five* adventure stories when she first came up with the winning formula in 1942, but after she received thousands of pleas for more, she increased it to twelve. But still readers were clamouring for more. By the time she decided to write the final instalment, twenty-one years later, Enid had sold a staggering 6 million books, and they have never been out of print since. As new generations continue to discover and follow the series, sales remain consistently high, with each title selling in the region of 60,000 copies a year even now. These sales figures show no signs of slowing down in Britain or abroad.

As the publishers started marketing toys, games and stationery featuring *The Famous Five* gang, Enid was often asked if they were based on real people she knew. She usually responded by claiming that she did not write about specific people or situations from real life, but admitted that she would unwittingly recognise certain qualities of someone she knew in a character she had created, although she always insisted it was a coincidence. Many people wanted to know who inspired the best-loved character George, an androgynous girl who acted like a boy and longed to be one of them. There was constant speculation that she was in fact a version of Enid, and many years later while promoting *The Famous Five* in France, she finally confessed in a rare unguarded moment to her foreign agent Rosica Cohn that indeed she had actually based George on herself. Enid never liked discussing her own upbringing, either in public or in private, but George was a clear reflection of her as a child.

In her memoirs Enid glossed over the true inspiration for the character:

> Yes, George is real, but she is grown up now. She had a dog, of course, and the real George was short haired, freckled, sturdy and snub nosed. She was bold and daring, hot tempered and loyal. She was sulky as George is too, but she isn't now. We grew out of those failings – or we should! Do you like George? I do.

George, a passionate tomboy who could out-swim, out-climb and outwit any boy, refused to conform to any gender stereotypes and has become a powerful role model for millions of young girls. George always seemed angry, seething with resentment that she had not been born a boy, and when her cousin Anne really wanted to insult her – in rare moments of spite – she knew just what to say: 'They're real boys, not pretend boys like you.' To most readers George remains the most popular of Enid's creations. The contrast between her behaviour and Anne's traditional femininity only made her appear all the more subversive.

It also emerged that Bill Cunningham, a character that appeared in all eight of the *Adventure* series, was based on a real person too, an amusing man she had met on holiday at a hotel in Swanage years earlier. He had asked her to put him in one of her books 'bald head and all' and jokingly suggested she call him Bill Smugs of the Secret Service. He did indeed appear as an important character called Smugs. Another recurring character in the fifteen *Mystery* series was Police Inspector Jenks, who Enid based on Stephen Jennings, a cheerful local officer who had been friends with Hugh when he was organising the Home Guard years earlier. Enid sought his advice when she was working on stories that involved aspects of police procedure, and when she asked if he would mind appearing as a kindly inspector who was a great friend to the sleuthing children, he cheerfully agreed. Jennings was delighted when he read the stories and discovered Enid had promoted him to Superintendent, since she tended to portray police as bungling buffoons. Her other famous fictional officer Mr Goon was pompous, stupid and often outwitted by the children solving mysteries and crimes in *The Five Find-Outers* series.

As well as sometimes using people she knew, Enid would also recycle anecdotes from her own childhood, or amusing stories recounted to her by other parents. One of her former editors at Brockhampton Press, Ewart Wharmby, helped inspire the idea for the *Secret Seven* series after telling Enid how his four children had formed their own little club with strict rules and a password. He described the headquarters they had created in a garden shed, prompting Enid to write to Wharmby's eldest son asking for more details, sending him in return enough money to buy 'jelly and chips' for his club. It was a bargain since she made a fortune from the fifteen *Secret Seven* books she wrote in rapid succession between 1949 and 1963. There was however a moment of discomfort when Enid abbreviated the gang's initials to SS just four years after the end of the Second World War. Hitler's sinister political soldiers, the Schutzstaffel, had been known as the SS, but she unthinkingly wrote: 'At school they all wore their little badges with SS embroidered on the button. It was fun to see the other children looking enviously at them wishing they could have one too.'

The Secret Seven were younger than *The Famous Five*, but equally clever and fearless. In each book George, Pam, Barbara, Colin, Jack and their dog Scamper would meet in the shed at Peter and Janet's house, having been alerted to a mystery that needed to be solved, often by hearing news of a theft or an unusual character spotted lurking in the area. In the first instalment *The Secret Seven* discovered that two strange old men were hiding a stolen racehorse in a deserted house nearby and attempting to dye its coat so they could race it under a new name. As always their snooping was dangerous but in a good cause and their ingenuity and goodness saved the day. Even when their parents discovered that their children had been out all night confronting hardened criminals, they expressed only pride and admiration for their achievements. They never seemed to mind the children getting tangled up with criminals and the police were always grateful for their help. Like *The Famous Five* series, the stories were a winning combination of risky adventure and the routine of ordinary life. The crimebusters still had to tidy their bedrooms, finish their homework and mind their manners, but were given enviable amounts of freedom and independence too. A small handful of working class characters made appearances in the series, such as Larry the mechanic who spoke to the children in cockney expletives including 'Cor!' and 'Lovaduck!'. Since they were aimed at slightly younger children than *The Famous Five*, the language was even more simplistic, and at one point Enid even went so far as to explain an ambulance as 'The van that ill people are taken to hospital in'. But there were no complaints from readers who devoured updates about characters they felt they knew. And it did not seem to matter that yet again the children were travelling to farms or islands far from home to track down treasure, smugglers, spies or kidnappers.

Many critics complained that Enid displayed snobbish attitudes towards class. In *Five Fall Into Adventure*, published in 1950, some papers were stolen from Uncle Quentin's study by a gypsy tomboy called Jo who was used by her brutal father in the robbery and an attempt to kidnap George and Timmy. Jo's father was in cahoots with 'foreign agents' but the gang outwitted him. When they first spotted Jo and her father on the beach she was described as 'a dirty little ragamuffin' and Dick said to Julian: 'I hope they don't come near us. I feel as if I can smell them from here.' Dick went on to hit Jo, before realising she was in fact a girl. Later, once the gang had turned the agents in to the police and Jo was deserted by her father, she was given a good scrubbing and some new clothes. Once she conformed she could be adopted by the cook's cousin and allowed to enter their rosy world.

It was argued that Enid placed too much emphasis on people looking a certain way in order to gain entry into their judgemental middle-class environment, and the character of Jo provided a perfect opportunity for the privileged characters to exert their superiority and charity. Working class characters only appeared in Enid's stories as criminals, figures of fun, submissive to their masters, disliked, immoral or stupid. But in *The Child and The Book*, Nicholas Tucker praised the action-packed nature of Enid's most popular books, which he said promoted literacy and were a good way for children to start reading and understanding long chapter books by themselves. He said that adults needlessly took against the stories, deeming them inferior when they should just be glad children were reading at all. He wrote: 'Her plots forge ahead almost in an ecstasy of action. It is untrue to imagine they were always easily predictable; the excitement and happy ending may have been, but not the details in between, and to that extent she can keep even the most sceptical adult reader uncertain until the last few pages.'

Tucker pointed out that the idea of adults censoring children's reading choices is riddled with hypocrisy since they have the freedom themselves to read whatever they wish. He added that what children like and what they ought to have were often two very different things, and it was unrealistic to expect children's literature to:

> avoid any reflection of its audience's immaturity, even when such reflections may sometimes seem crude and perhaps unfeeling. If all children's authors consistently write above the heads of their audience, and if the institutions which provide books for the young become over-fastidious in their selections, rather than children themselves changing, children's literature itself could become increasingly remote from those for whom it is meant to be catering.

Tucker also noted an unrealistic lack of sexual tension between a group of youngsters aged between 12 and 17. Romance was never high on Enid's agenda, mostly because it would have slowed down the pace of her fast-moving plots.

Enid has often been seen as one of the first authors to write about children as detectives, solving crimes without the aid of adults, but she had been inspired years earlier when she was teaching in Suffolk by Erich Kastner's *Emil and the Detectives* which had been a very popular book at the time. First published in 1929, it told the story of Emil Tischbein who was robbed on a train bound for Berlin of the money which he was delivering from his hardworking mother to his needy relatives. A gang of boys helped him chase, capture and finally unmask the thief who turned out to be a bank robber wanted by the police. It was thought to be one of the first classic detective stories aimed at children, and there are certainly similarities between this story and Enid's series *The Five Find-Outers*. The protagonists of *The Five Find-Outers*, Larry, Pip, Daisy, Bets, Fatty and his dog called Buster, first appeared in *The Mystery of Burnt Cottage*, published in 1943, trying to deduce who set fire to a local property. It proved so popular that there were eventually fifteen stories in the series, although many adults condemned the way the children were rude and even spiteful to the bungling policeman Mr Goon, who they nicknamed 'Clear Orf'. In *The Mystery of the Secret Room*, Enid wrote: 'Clear-Orf was the village policeman Mr Goon, detested by the children. He in turn detested them, especially as twice they had managed to solve problems before he himself had. No one had seen Mr Goon. Nobody particularly wanted to. He was not an amiable person at all, with his fat red face and bulging frog eyes.' While it was unlike Enid personally to show contempt for law and order, it was yet another example of her seeing the world through the eyes of children.

This series was soon followed by *The Rockingdown Mystery*, published in 1949, which has since been viewed as one of Enid's most sophisticated series of books. They followed her tried and tested formula of a group of children – Diana, Roger, a mysterious boy called Barney and Snubby with his dog Loony – having unsupervised adventures while on holiday. Enid then said she wanted to change the name of her own dog Laddie because 'He really is such a lunatic sometimes!' Enid repeated the success of this established format with the best-selling *Adventure* series, nine books written between 1944 and 1955 about Jack, Lucy-Ann, Dinah and Philip who track down forgers, robbers and various other criminals during their school holidays. All these similar sounding series may appear repetitive and entirely predictable in terms of their plot, characterisations, structure and even the elements of mild jeopardy, but they sold in their millions because Enid understood that children wanted to read about other children from their own point of view, not from the standpoint of any adult.

In 1975 critic Gillian Avery explained their success:

> *Famous Five* and *Secret Seven* might have encountered every desperado on the Interpol calendar, but they know and we know that they are always perfectly safe. They can roam Dartmoor and tramp the fells in the calm certainty that when they are hungry and tired there will be a rosy-cheeked farmer's wife standing on her doorstep, waiting to welcome them with cream teas and put them to bed between lavender scented sheets. Everybody is their friend, except the criminals whom of course they will outwit.

Chapter Twelve

Enid had so many different projects on the go at the same time that it had become impossible for her to oversee all the different creative and production aspects of her books. It was a mammoth task, and while Enid would never admit she was overwhelmed, eventually she agreed to employ a literary agent. George Greenfield, who she hired in 1954, later told how he was astonished by Enid's 'card index' mind and how she had a remarkable ability to refer to specific sentences in letters she had dispatched months earlier, as well as recalling detailed clauses of contracts she had signed with various editors, publishers and lawyers. He had first been introduced to Enid in 1947 when he took over the running of one of her publishing companies, Werner Laurie, part of the Hatchards group. He did not work with many women at the time but they struck up an immediate rapport. From the start George was impressed with Enid's clear understanding of the business world, and over time she grew to trust him implicitly to represent her to a number of different publishers who were clamouring to print whatever Enid Blyton books they could get their hands on. Her name equalled big money and she was juggling increasingly lucrative offers which George handled smoothly on her behalf. He was a highly intelligent man but sensitive and understanding to Enid's personal needs too and they enjoyed a successful working relationship for many years. He would be by her side throughout numerous complex negotiations about plays, films or any new books.

Enid was very fond of George and always looked forward to meeting him as they would talk mostly about the world of books, rather than the financial and legal matters that were fast building up around her. Books were his passion too and they shared a determination to make sure every one was produced as well as possible. The bond between them was purely professional, although Kenneth was rarely invited to join them. While George would visit Green Hedges from time to time, Kenneth felt he was interfering and far too close to his wife, so on the whole tended to avoid him. Regardless of Kenneth's animosity, Enid kept George on for many years. He was an important ally as he could be trusted to protect her independence, and was one of the few men involved in her business affairs who did not treat her as 'the little woman' unable to fully understand what they were discussing. Enid frequently encountered this attitude, which she found enormously irritating since she was actually a shrewd and competent businesswoman who usually made very wise and ruthless decisions when she needed to. Enid comprehended all aspects of marketing, branding and publicity. George treated her as an equal and their friendship was one of very few that continued for the rest of her life.

Generally the men at Enid's various publishing houses tended to find Kenneth rather rude and could not understand why he appeared so indifferent. In fact, his deafness was a major stumbling block when it came to social interactions, but as a scientist Kenneth found little common ground with people in publishing, and preferred to leave Enid to it. He was quite content to pass his time playing golf, and spent her money rather ostentatiously, which meant her financial advisors tended to have little respect for him. Enid had been persuaded that it made sound business sense to form her own company to co-ordinate her increasingly complex contracts and finances, and to shoulder much of the administrative burden, which was distracting her from writing. She established and became chair of Darrell Waters Limited, with Kenneth also on the board of directors; Gillian would join years later, following a career in children's publishing during which she edited a magazine called *Blue Moon*. The original board members included Enid's solicitor Arnold Thirlby, accountant John Basden and financial advisor Eric Rogers who ran the company day to day and oversaw investment opportunities for Enid's ever growing fortune. She and Eric met regularly for lunch at the Savoy Hotel in London, which he jokingly referred to as his local pub. At first Kenneth was suspicious of Eric's motives, and believed he might be wheeling and dealing with his wife's hard-earned money, and the board meetings could be hostile affairs, but over time the two men came to enjoy each other's company a great deal as they shared an interest in horse racing. Eric worked closely with Enid's personal solicitor Harold Rubenstein, who also became a good friend over the years, as his professional attitude meant Enid felt comfortable revealing personal information about herself without risking her reputation and credibility.

While she was content to hand over the running of her financial affairs to the company, Enid still insisted on close involvement in her charitable endeavours. She had been encouraging donations to children's charities for over twenty years, which the board was happy for her to continue doing, but it was a different matter when it came to giving away vast sums of her own personal fortune. Enid felt deeply compassionate towards children with disabilities but the board did not like the idea of her donating royalties from books to good causes, and in the end Enid became so frustrated at being prevented from giving money as she had always done that she resigned from her own company at the end of 1954. Shortly afterwards she paid a visit to Harold Rubenstein to draw up a will to ensure that her requests to continue supporting the charities close to her heart would be honoured after her death. Sadly that will was later lost and the directors wrote a new will for her to sign when she was suffering serious mental health problems shortly before she died.

Setting up the company also led to a happy reconciliation with Enid's old friend Dorothy Richards, because years earlier Dorothy had been chosen to act as the trustee of some bonds which had been purchased for Gillian and Imogen and had now matured so they needed to contact her again. Enid was delighted to welcome her old friend back to Green Hedges, but their relationship never again returned to its former intimacy. Imogen recalled:

> She and my mother laughed and joked as they had years before and she got on well with my stepfather. It cannot have been easy for her, settling back into a routine that she had left nearly ten years before. Although Dorothy had not altered, except to age a little, my mother had changed a great deal. A happy marriage and a successful career had removed the need for the old close friendship that they had shared before. My mother no longer had the time to share with her that she had in the old days. Almost every moment now was planned and ordered and Dorothy had to take back seat.

This time, Dorothy was more like an employee than a friend to Enid. Some observers remarked that she was almost like a royal lady in waiting, acting as a personal assistant during public appearances, sitting behind Enid in her box at the theatre, or patiently listening without really offering an opinion of her own. Throughout her life Enid struggled with forming enduring friendships, and although she may not have liked to admit it for fear it would be seen as a weakness, she did need someone to confide in. While she never actually had therapy sessions in the traditional sense, Enid did regularly send long letters to psychologist Peter McKellar. They corresponded at length for years, and she found an outlet to explain the complex workings of her mind as well as her highly unusual writing process. She told him:

> I shut my eyes for a few minutes, with my portable typewriter on my knee; I make my mind a blank and wait – and then, as clearly as I would see real children my characters stand before me in my mind's eye. I see them in detail – hair, eyes, feet, clothes, expression. More than that, I know their characters. They take on movement and life – they talk and laugh (I hear them). That's enough for me and I begin. The first sentence comes straight into my mind, I don't have to think of it – I don't have to think of anything. The story is enacted almost as if I had a private cinema screen there.

Enid added that she was in the unique position of not only being the author of her stories, but also being able to read them for the first time as if someone else had come up with the ideas. And, bizarrely, since she claimed the characters she created took on minds and personalities of their own, she would sometimes find herself laughing out loud at their jokes as if she had never heard them before: 'Sometimes a character makes a joke, a really funny one that makes me laugh as I type it on my paper, and I think: "Well I couldn't have thought of that myself in a hundred years!" And then I think: "Well, who did think of it?"'

Enid explained her creative style further in her memoirs *The Story of My Life*, telling her readers:

> If I sit in my chair and shut my eyes for a minute or two, in comes the story I am waiting for, all ready and complete in my imagination. I sit in my chair and think, 'Now today I am going to begin a new book. What shall it be? Adventure? Circus? Nature? Fairy Tale? Mystery? I think it is time for a fairy tale! A fairy tale it shall be!'
>
> I have to find two things when I write a book. I have to find my characters, of course, and the setting for the story – the place where everything happens. So I shut my eyes and I look into my mind's eye. You know what that is, don't you? We all have one. The story comes out complete and whole from beginning to end. If I tried to think out or invent the whole book, I could not do it. For one thing, it would bore me, and for another, it would lack the 'verve' and the extraordinary touches and surprising ideas that flood out

from my imagination. People in my books make jokes I could never have thought of myself. I am merely a sightseer, a reporter, and interpreter.

When children asked Enid how she wrote so quickly, as they did frequently, she attempted to explain the same theory to them too, that she imagined she was watching a film, and typing as fast as she could to keep up with all the action and dialogue she was seeing in front of her. She also confided to McKellar in another letter that most of her stories were inspired by or based upon her own experiences:

> I think my imagination contains all the things I have ever seen or heard, things my conscious mind has long since forgotten. And they have been jumbled about till a light penetrates into the mass, and a happening here or an object there is taken out, transmuted, or formed into something that takes a natural and rightful place in the story – I may recognise it or I may not – I don't think that I use anything I have not seen or experienced – I don't think I could. Our books are facets of ourselves. It is open to all writers to enrich their imagination and to make it easy of access. The more one observes and hears and learns, the more one reads and ponders and muses consciously on this, that and the other, the richer the imagination becomes.

One of the many remarkable things about Enid was that she could write an entire book in one sitting, stopping only when she was forced to take breaks to eat and sleep. She could have written even more than the 8,000–10,000 words she managed some days: 'If only my arms didn't get tired of being poised over my typewriter,' she explained, adding that she did not get mentally tired because she was only using her imagination: 'Brain work is tiring. Using one's imagination is not,' she explained.

Enid found herself the butt of many jokes as this extraordinary process was mocked by commentators who found her apparent theory implausible to say the least. Popular comedienne Joyce Grenfell sent up Enid in an amusing sketch from 1954. She said:

> Hullo boys and girls. I was so pleased when you asked me to come along and tell you how I write my books for children. Well, of course, the answer is – I don't. No, my books write themselves for

me. Well, as you know children, I write lots and lots of books for you and this is how I set about it. First of all I go upstairs to my Hidey Hole – well, this is really just a great big upstairs workroom but I like to call it my Hidey Hole. I pin a notice on the door and it says: 'Gone to Make Believe Land.' This is just my way of saying: 'Please don't come in and bother me because a book is writing itself for me and we mustn't disturb it must we?'

Then I put a clean white sheet of paper in my typewriter and I sit down in front of it and I close my eyes. And what do I see? I see a rambling old house in Cornwall. And I hear seagulls – and I see children – one – two – three children scrambling up the cliffs because they are very nearly late for tea, and their names are Jennifer-Ann, and Robin-John, and the little one is called Midge – because he is the littlest one. (Oh yes, he has a proper name. It's Anthony Timothy Jeremy Michael and he doesn't like porridge – but we won't tell anyone will we?)

Regardless of the mockery she endured, her unique process was the only way Enid knew how to work and it was certainly successful. Her workload may have seemed overwhelming to others, but somehow Enid always appeared to be coping well and never cracked under the strain of it all. When asked to explain why she produced such a high volume of work, Enid insisted her output was nothing out of the ordinary: 'It is not usual for one author to produce such a number of books,' she said. 'Nor is it usual to produce such a variety. Authors tend to keep to one subject, and, where children are concerned, to one age of child only. But my difficulty is, and has always been, that I love all ages of children from babyhood to adolescence.'

Enid did have to streamline her other work to allow time for all the fiction, and seven years after giving up her *Teacher's World* column, Enid also stopped editing *Sunny Stories* in 1952, withdrawing after twenty-six years at the helm of the magazine. But she would never dream of letting down her readers, she felt she owed them a great debt, so let it be known that she planned to start production on her own new fortnightly magazine. Enid not only intended to be the editor of the *Enid Blyton Magazine*, but would also write the entire contents herself too. It came as no surprise to anyone, especially those at the publishing company Evans Brothers, that the magazine was an instant success.

Enid was a great admirer of the young Princess Elizabeth who was due to take the throne in 1952 following the unexpected death of her father King

Enid working at Green Hedges. (Alamy)

Enid's birthplace in Dulwich, commem-
orated with a blue plaque on the wall.

The entrance to the housing development which now stands on the site of Enid's former home,
Green Hedges near Beaconsfield in Buckinghamshire.

Corfe Castle in Dorset, the inspiration for Kirrin Castle in the *Famous Five* series.

Purbeck in Dorset where Enid and Kenneth spent many of their holidays and bought their own golf course.

Enid Blyton.

The entire collection of twenty-one Famous Five titles (minus the 11th), belonging to the author.

The controversial black golliwog doll, belonging to the author.

Enid at work in her private library at Green Hedges, surrounded by copies of her own work.

To commemorate the centenary of her birth, the Royal Mail issued a set of stamps featuring Noddy, her most famous creation.

Enid Blyton's *Noddy*

Old Thatch, the family home Enid and her first husband Hugh Pollock bought together in Buckinghamshire.

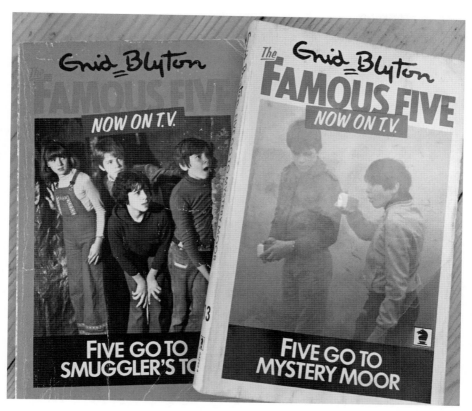

Reprinted *Famous Five* covers that were produced when the stories were developed into
television programmes. (Author)

Southernhay, the house in Surrey where Enid ran a small school. The blue plaque commemorates the time she lived there between 1920 and 1924.

George VI, and decided to launch her new publication in the run up to the Coronation. Enid cleverly timed the early issues to capture the great national excitement and sense of pride in the royal family with a six-part story called 'The Story of Our Queen', and a special photographic competition, giving children the unique opportunity to win seats to watch the Coronation. When Enid was informed a few months later that the new Queen Elizabeth II herself was a fan, she urged her readers to send Christmas wishes and personal messages of 'affection and loyalty' to the monarch. Enid received hundreds of messages and carefully selected twelve, which were printed in a special leather bound volume, along with a letter from Enid herself, and sent to Buckingham Palace where they were received with great enthusiasm.

The magazine wielded phenomenal power, which Enid used as a way of raising money for various charities, encouraging her young readers to support causes aimed at helping other children and animals. Eager to impress Enid, devoted children across the world would organise sales, concerts and fetes and send her the proceeds. The most popular of her chosen charities was the People's Dispensary for Sick Animals, which Enid regularly mentioned in her columns, and was selected as a beneficiary of The Busy Bee Club, which grew so fast it gathered over 100,000 members in its first three years and soon had its own publication, *The Busy Bees News.*

Children responded well to being members of such organisations, leading to the creation of The Famous Five Club, in response to massive demand from her regular readers. By this time Hodder & Stoughton were publishing at least one new title about the four adventurous children and their dog every year. Enid gave her permission for the club on the condition that funds would be raised for the Shaftesbury Society Babies Home in Beaconsfield, a local charity which cared for deprived infants from the East End of London. Enid already supported the home financially as a member of the committee, and as chair from 1954 until it closed in 1967. She made regular visits, taking toys and sweets for the children, as well as fresh produce from her garden. Enid also signed over thousands of pounds worth of the publishing royalties from *Before I Go To Sleep*, a book of Bible stories and prayers, which bought the equipment for a special Famous Five Ward, a new playground, building extensions, theatre trips and Christmas parties for children at the home.

And after she wrote about a particularly emotionally charged visit she made to one of the Sunshine Homes for Blind Babies, her readers set up The Sunbeam Society, and within 6 years its distinctive yellow badge showing a blind baby with its head turned towards the sun was being worn by over 22,000 readers. And when Enid encouraged readers to support a special centre for children suffering from cerebral palsy in Chelsea in 1955, their response was once again to set up another fundraising club which had furnished a new hostel by the start of 1957. Evans Brothers had predicted a success but they were astounded by Enid's pulling power and threw a party for the children who were running the clubs to meet her at Montague House, the company's central London office. By the time she eventually closed the magazine in 1960, membership of The Enid Blyton Magazine Club was well over 150,000 children from all over the world. During the six years it was published, the magazine managed to raise a staggering £35,000 for a number of good causes. It was an amount, Enid told her readers, 'even grown-ups would find difficult to raise'. Enid had become famous for her dedication to the worthy causes close to her heart, and for always encouraging her readers to be kind to anyone less fortunate than themselves. Several of the clubs continued even without the magazine and The Enid Blyton Society still thrives to this day, making hefty donations to children's hospitals including Great Ormond Street in London and Stoke Mandeville in Aylesbury.

Her writing schedule was relentless, but Enid found herself much in demand to make personal appearances at schools, libraries and bookshops up and down the country, and she became well known as a charismatic speaker who could easily control large crowds of children and adults alike, holding them spellbound and silent as they absorbed every word she said. She was also considered something of an expert on childcare and education, and spoke out in the press on a number of controversial issues including the new demand for women to take on traditionally male jobs. The heavy loss of life during both world wars meant women were needed to replace men in factories, but Enid felt it was leaving too many children separated from their mothers.

Despite being the main bread winner in her own family, and the fact that she had banished her children's father from their home, Enid was against women going out to work and had surprisingly traditional views of a mother's role. She said:

> Spoilt children are selfish, complaining and often conceited. But whose fault is that? It is the mother, always the mother, that makes the home. The father does his share, he holds the reins too – but it is the mother who makes a happy, contented home. She is the centre of it. She should always be there to welcome the children home, to see them and listen to them. I was lucky to have a gift that could be used at home. I could not have left my husband or my

children and gone out into the world to make my career. All true mothers will know what I mean when I say that.

Enid felt so strongly about families staying together that she was invited to give a speech at the opening of an exhibition of 'mothercraft' at Central Hall in Westminster in November 1949, which she knew would be widely covered in the press. She took the opportunity to make a rare foray into the world of politics which she had until this point avoided. Enid criticised the government's call for married women to work in factories, following the great losses of soldiers. 'This would mean abandoning children to the care of others,' she insisted.

And despite the struggles with her personal faith, Enid had equally firmly held opinions when it came to the spiritual welfare of children. Enid used the pages of her new magazine to urge her young readers to follow a daily course of Bible readings. Renewing her friendship with Dorothy had reignited Enid's former interest in religion, and in an article she wrote for the *Church of England Newspaper* Enid explained her newfound zeal saying: 'I want to take up the whip that Jesus once used when he drove from the Temple the polluters of holiness and goodness in the hearts of children.'

She decided that attending church regularly and learning from the Bible was a vital part of every child's education: 'Religious teaching provides a moral backbone throughout life;' she wrote. 'It gives a child invincible weapons with which to fight any evils, any problems he meets.' In one of her many articles for the Church of England newspaper, Enid wrote furiously about violence in films, the evil of child murderers and the government's plans to abolish capital punishment. She insisted that children wanted to read about action, adventures and animals, not watch gruesome tales of murder, torture or ghosts. Enid was only too aware of the pressure on her as a role model for children, and ensured her characters always had a strong moral compass, and good always triumphed over evil. She had no interest in scaring her readers and felt films such as *Snow White and the Seven Dwarves* were too frightening for sensitive children. She believed they should be told 'happy and cheerful stories' and the family units she created were always cosy ones in the end. Enid was utterly confident that she truly understood precisely what it was that her readers expected: 'My public, bless them, feel in my books a sense of security, an anchor, a sure knowledge that right is right, and that such things as courage and kindness deserve to be emulated,' she wrote. 'Naturally the morals or ethics are intrinsic to that story – and therein lies their power.'

Chapter Thirteen

With both girls settled at boarding school, Kenneth was starting to think it might be a good time to retire, and strongly urged his wife to do the same. But Enid was busier than ever and had just come up with an idea for a new adventure story called *Six Cousins of Mistletoe Farm* when she was forced to stop work for the first time in years, but not out of choice. In October 1947 Imogen developed infantile paralysis in her left leg and was rushed to Great Ormond Street Hospital in London for emergency treatment after contracting an infection during their annual summer holiday to Swanage. There was some confusion over the initial diagnosis, and when Enid took the call from Imogen's school she was terrified for her 12-year-old daughter, since there had been a widespread outbreak of polio at the time. Kenneth came into his own and quickly took charge of the situation, finding a private room for Imogen at the hospital where a second diagnosis revealed that she did indeed have polio. Although she was immediately given a lumbar puncture to remove the spinal fluid, the outlook was as dire as Enid first feared. Despite the gravity of the situation, Enid hated to be thought of as unprofessional and found the time to explain to her publisher Noel Evans that there would be a slight delay in delivering her work on time:

> I shall simply have to put my work on one side for a few weeks and be with her morning and afternoon in her private ward till I see how things go. So I must warn you that I do not see my way at the moment to getting the book done as soon as I hoped. I am dreadfully sorry but I am a bit knocked over at the moment – it's so awful to see one's own child attacked like this though I am hoping it will be one of the milder attacks and that it has been diagnosed early enough for us to prevent any damage.

Imogen had to stay in hospital for several months, after being moved from Great Ormond Street to Kenneth's ward at St Stephen's for physiotherapy to help her walk again. She eventually made a full recovery, and was home in time for Christmas. Enid was aware that her younger brother Carey was also dangerously ill with polio at the same time, but she did not visit him and without access to the expensive care Imogen received, he was left paralysed. Yet when Enid heard that the son of Paul Hodder-Williams, her publisher at Hodder & Stoughton, had contracted the same illness too she sent him a parcel of books and a kind personal letter.

While Imogen recuperated, she spent more time with her mother than she had done in years. She was allowed to help Enid come up with names for the horses in *Six Cousins of Mistletoe Farm*. Since she loved riding, Imogen wrote detailed descriptions of each animal too. When the book was finally published, it was dedicated to Imogen, and she was credited for her contribution. Enid also took Imogen on a shopping spree at Harrods, the exclusive department store, where she was also kitted out in new uniform for Benenden School in Kent. Both she and Gillian had settled into the new school much better than they had at Godstowe, and found their relationship with Enid improved as they got older. Enid and Kenneth would sometimes drive down to Kent in their new Rolls Royce and stay at an inn in Goudhurst, and take Imogen and her friends out for lunch: 'My mother wrote to me, short friendly letters, much the same as the ones she wrote to her fans,' she said later. Enid often appeared in the press, but urged staff at the school to shield her daughters from any reports that they might find upsetting, so they would sometimes discover copies of newspapers with articles already cut out if they had been mentioned. In one interview with the *Daily Express*, Enid told the journalist Nancy Spain that her daughter's adolescent problems tended to go away if they were ignored – which seemed to sum up Enid's attitude to almost everything she found difficult or unpleasant.

Kenneth had not given up on his plans for a peaceful retirement, and he wanted to travel abroad and play more sport. They were both excellent tennis players, and had a hard court built at Green Hedges, but Kenneth preferred golf. Even before she learnt how to play properly, Enid was so devoted to her second husband that she would patiently walk around the course with him. Once she started taking lessons, with her usual gusto, Enid soon achieved an impressive handicap of eighteen, and in 1951 she bought her own eighteen-hole golf course at Studland Bay in Dorset. Kenneth was very involved in improving and developing the run down golf course which needed a great deal of renovation work when they first bought it. From then on they spent as much time there as they could, taking at least three golfing holidays a year, usually staying for two weeks at a time at the Grand Hotel overlooking Poole Harbour, and became so friendly with their caddy Johnny

James that he inspired the groundsman character Lucas in *Five Have a Mystery To Solve*.

Enid loved the area, and even if she did not have time to play a round of golf with Kenneth, she would sit on the hillside overlooking Poole Harbour while she worked. Those trips tended to be the only way Enid would actually switch off from her writing and properly relax. She liked to keep fit and slim, and was proud of her ability to touch her toes until well into her sixties. Since the children were very young, they had always stayed at the nearby Grosvenor Hotel, but Enid switched to the Grand when the girls were in their teens and were caught taking a late-night swim with a party of students who were working as waiters at the hotel that summer. Kenneth made a furious complaint to the management and Enid felt the girls had disgraced themselves. Embarrassed and fearful for her reputation, Enid vowed to never return to the hotel.

With Enid's income soaring to well over £100,000 a year, they certainly did not need any more money and could live the rest of their lives in the lap of luxury even if Enid never earnt another penny. They employed a number of staff including a cook, maid and chauffeur to drive their fleet of cars – Enid had upgraded her old black Rover with a rabbit on the front to an expensive collection which included a Bentley, a Rolls Royce and an MG saloon sports car. She avoided public transport entirely, and took taxis between meetings in London if she needed to. She never particularly enjoyed driving as she found it an unwelcome distraction from being allowed to let her imagination wander freely. Enid was most thrilled when she realised she was wealthy enough to no longer need to shop in Debenhams, and opened an account at Harrods as soon as she could afford it. To Enid the Knightsbridge department store was a magical place, and her visits would usually last all day. She would have her hair done and treat herself to lunch in the restaurant. She loved the furniture department, and started to accumulate pieces of reproduction walnut Queen Anne furniture, as well as choosing new pieces of china and glass. She bought all the children's Christmas and birthday presents from the toy department, and was as excited as they were by the music and pet departments. She would hold book signings and storytelling sessions in the book department. Afterwards she would take a taxi to meet Kenneth at St Stephen's Hospital and they would be driven home together in the Rolls Royce. Occasionally Kenneth would join her on one of these shopping sprees, particularly if she was planning to buy something very expensive like a fur coat.

With money to spare, Enid also treated them to a black and white television set in time to watch the 1948 Olympic Games, and Kenneth would spend hours smoking cigars and watching sport, especially horse racing every Saturday, and placed regular bets with some success. But Enid never really liked watching television. She found it unnecessary since her vivid imagination kept her entertained, and television moved too slowly in comparison. Kenneth's hearing was getting worse and he found it increasingly difficult to join in games of bridge or dinner parties. They rarely entertained other couples at home, and if his colleagues from the hospital visited they tended not to bring their wives. Enid never minded being the only woman at the table, as she was used to it during business meetings, and she enjoyed being the centre of attention and always made an effort to look glamorous. As was the tradition of the time, Enid would excuse herself at the end of the meal to happily wait alone in the drawing room while the men drank port. Kenneth enjoyed selecting expensive wine to serve at these occasions and Enid, who had never really liked drinking before, gradually learnt to share his tastes if they had company, and she would pour herself a sherry before lunch and gin before dinner. She also served brandy and liqueurs after dinner.

Enid did all she could to accommodate Kenneth, and even accompanied him on regular visits with him to see his mother, a fearsome woman who intimidated Enid somewhat and lived to the ripe old age of 104. She also made an effort to make friends with Kenneth's sister Margery, his brother Hugh and niece Sheelagh, which was surprising since she had no contact at all with the family of her first husband, or indeed any of her own relatives. But Kenneth still longed to travel, and while Enid enjoyed staying in hotels, she had no interest in leaving the country, and never understood the point of foreign holidays. However, after they invited their next door neighbours Gordon and Ida Biggs to join them in Swanage, the couple suggested in return that they all take a rather exotic sounding trip to New York. Enid was not at all keen on the idea, according to Imogen: 'She was afraid of change and new experiences that might expose her.' But Kenneth managed to persuade her and in the autumn of 1948 they set sail on a three-week cruise across the Atlantic Ocean. Their ship, the *Queen Elizabeth*, was of course very luxurious but Enid did not like the lack of privacy, she was shy in crowds and found the familiarity rather intrusive. Needless to say, Enid buried herself in work. She could not bring herself to stop working for that long anyway, so she used the trip as an opportunity to meet American publishers, booksellers, librarians and reviewers. She spoke at several events while she was there since she had won a Boys Club of America award for best junior book published the year before, and Enid seized the opportunity to promote herself further in the US. She received an enthusiastic welcome when the *Queen Elizabeth* docked in Manhattan. The *New York Times* described Enid as 'A bright-eyed, breathless Englishwoman' and when she was asked the secret of her success in an interview, Enid told the newspaper: 'All is takes, really, is imagination.'

Enid said afterwards: 'I learnt more in ten days over there than I would have learnt in ten years here,' but her visit did not boost sales in the US, and she could never be lured out of the country again, and all her future holidays from then on were taken in Dorset. And shortly after returning from that trip, Enid decided that they would no longer be friends with the Biggs family. She insisted that the gap in the hedge that the children had used to run between the houses must be closed up, and Imogen was told she could not continue to be friends with their son Keith any longer. There was no explanation for her sudden change of heart, although there was a rumour that it had something to do with roulette parties which the Biggs held at their house, gambling for small stakes. Ida Biggs had also given Imogen her first bra, although it was too large and had to be returned, it may have been deemed an inappropriate gesture. Very soon after the falling out the Biggs family sold their house and moved away from the area.

Enid also called an abrupt halt to their friendship with another couple who ran nearby riding stables which the girls would visit regularly to groom and ride the horses. Imogen spent most of the school holidays there, and eventually Enid bought her favourite horse, called Lucy Glitters. But once again there was no explanation for the apparent dispute with the owners, Mr and Mrs Gilbert, although Imogen later recalled: 'I used to hear her grumbling to my stepfather about my constant visits there. And once there was a bitter row between her and Mrs Gilbert over some aspect of my behaviour that she blamed on the Gilberts.' Enid was a household name by this time, at the height of her fame, and often felt that people struck up friendships with her and Kenneth because they were flattered by the attentions of someone so well known. As soon as she became suspicious of their motives Enid would immediately distance herself from anyone who might be deemed inappropriate, and her most lasting friendships were usually those based on successful working relationships.

Enid was finding time with the children easier as they grew up, and when they came home for the holidays brimming with amusing stories about their life at boarding school it gave Enid an idea. Her first attempt at writing about schools in the early 1950s was intended to have mass appeal, so she set *The Naughtiest Girl In The School* in a modern co-educational secondary school called Whyteleafe. The protagonist was a badly behaved pupil called Elizabeth Allen who tried to get into as much trouble as possible in the hope of being sent home, until she realised boarding school was the best place in the world. It was instantly popular with Enid's young fans and prompted three more books in the series, but her publishers at Methuen urged her to come up with a rather more conventional single-sex setting, with considerably better behaved pupils.

Enid did not waste any time and worked on producing two new series, *St Clare's* and *Malory Towers*, which were both set against a backdrop of more formal girls' schools where the new girls triumphed over adversity to become heroes by saving their friends from a scrape, usually scoring winning goals in lacrosse matches along the way, and gradually working their way up to becoming head girl. At the end of the series all the most popular girls headed off to university, at a time when women were expected to achieve little more than a good marriage. The books may have been somewhat less adventurous than Enid's earlier stories, but they were equally popular. Enid was asked many times if they were based on real schools, perhaps the ones she or her daughters had attended, but she always insisted they were a mix of various different places she had known. The tales Imogen and Gillian told their mother would bring back memories of her own school days, and she later told how much she liked to hear about: 'Games of lacrosse, hockey and tennis, the little spites and deceits of school life, the loyalty and generosities of friendship, and the never ending impact of one character on another.'

Enid may not have wanted to admit it publicly, but she knew that stories set in girls' boarding schools were so popular thanks in part to her predecessor Angela Brazil, who had already written a successful series of stories which became predominantly famous for the over the top exclamations her characters would use such as 'top hole!', 'a very jinky notion!' and 'what a bosomy idea!'. Her schoolgirls often had fervent crushes on other girls, and the amount of practical jokes and pranks they played on staff made the books unpopular with real life schoolteachers. In their 1976 book about girl's fiction, called *You're A Brick, Angela!*, literary critics Mary Cadogan and Patricia Craig echoed many parents and teachers when they suggested that Enid's plots were over simplified and crude: 'She is consistently trite. She writes down. Yet few children seem to resent this approach; the Enid Blyton combination of cosiness and excitement has proved almost irresistible, and parental disapproval and library bans have actually helped keep her books in circulation. Their popularity has never waned.' They added that the lack of ambiguity removed layers of meaning, making the stories easy to follow, since no individual character seemed to dominate more than any other and everyone was always on holiday or in the thick of the action. They also suggested that Enid won support for her characters by making their traits, even the negative ones such as laziness or bad tempers, appear attractive and entirely justifiable.

Another critic, Fred Inglis, pointed out that no matter how straightforward or basic a story was it would be popular if it was set in a boarding school environment, since the removal of parents made them seem attractive places to be. Most children did not notice or seem to mind about the class issue, the cost of boarding school fees was never mentioned, and the focus was always on friendships, which were celebrated in the end. In his book *The Promise of Happiness*, Inglis said that he had read Enid's stories himself as a child but unlike many other readers: 'Certainly took in from these books their overpowering snobbery, the meanness and vengefulness of so much of the morality, the herd victimisation of silliness and vanity. Reading Enid Blyton is much like reading comics. Awful, and indeed worse than comics, because so lacking in their lurid high spirits and loud vulgarity. Awful, but unimportant.' He concluded by stating that children only read Enid's books to avoid using their own imaginations.

But critics like him did Enid no harm. Most readers tended to celebrate and enjoy the sense of communal living space and shared rites of passage which she described in her school stories. While Enid wrote about three different schools – Whyteleafe, St Clare's and Malory Towers- they were all very similar environments and all the books focused on the behaviour of the pupils and small incidents that occurred between them over the course of an academic year. Although Whyteleafe was co-educational and the other two were for girls only, the format was the same. In each story the new pupils were immediately the centre of attention and were usually hot-headed or bad tempered, but eventually earned responsibility and popularity. The mean, dishonest and sneaky girls usually saw the error of their ways and learned from their mistakes. Anyone who broke the rules felt obliged to own up to their wrong doing, and got their come-uppance in the end in the form of a suitable punishment.

There was always the threat of the worst possible punishment of all – having to leave the school they adored, and the worst crime was letting the school down. In *Last Term At Malory Towers*, published in 1951, Enid wrote:

'"Shall I be expelled?" asked Deidre, panic stricken at the thought. "My father would be awfully upset. I haven't got a mother."' While the girls loved their parents they were all self-reliant and relationships with their friends were much more important than family.

Darrell, the plucky heroine of the *Malory Towers* series, was named after Kenneth and the fictional Darrell's father was also a surgeon like him. Just like all her most popular creations, she was outspoken, argumentative, not particularly feminine and never worried too much about her appearance – rather like Enid herself. As well as behaving like Enid, Darrell was an equally enthusiastic writer: 'Sally knew that the creative part had all been Darrell's,' she wrote about the heroine pulling off a triumphant theatrical performance. 'The words and the songs had all come out of Darrell's own imagination.'

The girls who spent too long looking in the mirror, smoothing down their dresses or tying ribbons in their hair were generally seen as silly and too perfect to be likeable. The most popular girls tended to come out with plenty of effervescent expletives – such as wizard, golly or gosh – especially during midnight feasts of treats like sardines, tinned pineapple and peppermint creams; and of course when someone scored the winning goal in a lacrosse match. At some point in all of Enid's school stories tensions were resolved with some form of raucous celebration. In *The Naughtiest Girl in The School* she wrote: 'Peals of laughter, roars of mirth, squeals and giggles filled the room from end to end. It did everyone good. Those gusts of laughter had cleared the air of all spitefulness, scorn and enmity. Everyone suddenly felt friendly and warm. It was good to be together to laugh and to play, to be friends.'

As in many of Enid's other stories, there were very few foreign characters in the school stories, and those that did make brief appearances were generally in need of charity or were treated with derision. In *Last Term At Malory Towers* Enid wrote: 'Suzanne was French. She hadn't quite the same ideas of responsibility that the British girls had.' Enid also showed her usual distain for working class people, or those who had come into money. In *The Twins at St Clare's* the character of Janet mocked Sheila's accent by saying: 'Hark at Sheila! Didn't ought to! Good heavens Sheila where were you brought up? Haven't you learnt by now that decent people don't say "Didn't ought to!" My goodness, you talk about your servants, and your Rolls Royce cars, your horse and your lake and goodness knows what else – and then you talk like the daughter of the dustman!' In *Malory*

Towers, Jo's wealthy father Mr Jones came in for similarly condescending treatment on account of the way he spoke:

> Jo once boasted that there wasn't anything her father couldn't buy. June had inquired whether he had enough money to buy himself a few hundred H's. Jo had never forgiven June for that. For the first time she had realised that her father's loud-voiced remarks were made all the worse by the way he continually dropped his H's and by his curious lapses in grammar.

Chapter Fourteen

Enid had quite a shock in 1945 when she discovered that she was pregnant, at the age of 48. Kenneth had always longed for a child and was thrilled, but because of her age he pleaded with Enid to slow down. For five months they allowed themselves to get excited about the new addition to their family, but when climbing a ladder to gather apples from a barn – which Kenneth had expressly forbidden her to do – Enid had a bad fall and lost the baby. Imogen was there but in her panic she ran away and hid, leaving her mother collapsed on the concrete floor. Kenneth rushed her to St Stephen's Hospital where his colleagues could treat her, but it was too late to save their son. Kenneth was devastated and was never able to talk about it, but Enid appeared bizarrely cheerful. True to form she refused to waste her valuable time mourning, as always she chose not to dwell on anything to do with death and mortality, and instead threw herself straight back into work with remarkable enthusiasm.

Later Imogen feared that Enid may have actually felt it was for the best that the child did not survive, given her age, and perhaps she had deliberately risked her pregnancy by climbing the ladder, which was a task she would usually have asked a servant to do: 'Could it possibly be that she had decided in her ruthless and practical way that the child should not be born?' Imogen wrote:

> She would have been aware of the high risk of giving birth to a child with a defect at her age; and her books were still the most important part of her life. Perhaps the real question is whether the birth of a son would have belatedly unlocked her mothering instinct. I, who let her down so completely, like to think that it would.

The Darrell Waters were dealt a further blow at the end of the 1940s when it emerged that they had failed to pay close enough attention to their business affairs and were given a nasty shock in the shape of a hefty tax bill. Since Enid was self-employed, the amount of tax she owed was estimated based on her income, and each year the estimate she submitted had stayed the same.

She did not make any major adjustments, even though her earnings had soared that decade. Her advisors knew that Enid had always taken care of her own accounts, although she did not like wasting time filling in forms, and had no interest in maths or figures. Eventually a tax inspector noticed that the famous Enid Blyton must surely be making more money than she admitted to, and launched an investigation into her financial affairs. It quickly became clear that she had failed to pay a huge chunk of what she owed over the past few years, and Enid was slapped with an enormous bill demanding all the unpaid tax and the Inland Revenue imposed large fines.

There was no way round it, but determined not to sacrifice the lifestyle that she and Kenneth were used to, Enid needed to raise money fast, and she knew exactly how to do it. Those post-war years had seen many families being reunited, and with soldiers finally returning from the war, the early 1950s saw a baby boom. Enid decided to capture the national mood and write more for very young children, specifically those under 7. With that bill looming over her she started to look around for inspiration with relish. One of her publishers, David White from Sampson Low, Marston and Company Ltd, suggested she write stories to accompany some unusual drawings he had been sent from a Dutch artist called Harmsen van der Beek. Enid loved Van Der Beek's illustrations of lively little people surrounded by distinctive houses and shops, fields of bluebells and large trees the moment she laid eyes on them. The Continental style scenes appealed hugely to Enid's imagination and White persuaded the artist to travel to England so they could meet. Although the lonely widower who had lost his wife during the Nazi occupation of Holland spoke almost no English, they hired an interpreter and soon struck up a great rapport. Both equally excited by the collaboration, together Enid and Harmsen set about designing a central character. Enid clearly described a quaint toy figure she could see in her mind's eye – a wooden puppet wearing a long hat, topped with a bell, over tousled hair, and as she talked Harmsen worked enthusiastically with his pencils, bringing her words to life.

By the end of that first meeting they both knew precisely what Noddy would look like. They also sketched out detailed images for other key characters including Big Ears the Pixie and the motherly figure of Mrs Tubby, as well as fleshing out the appearance of pixies, goblins and their toadstool houses. Enid was so impressed by what she called 'his particular genius' that she could not wait to start writing. Her publishers were astounded to receive the first four Noddy books just four days later. It was a fast turnaround even by Enid's standards, but they did not disappoint.

She also sent her manuscripts to Harmsen who was thrilled with the stories and responded enthusiastically to his new colleague, predicting a bright future ahead for them both:

> I have thoroughly enjoyed reading them and think they are extraordinary amusing, especially for an illustrator, because every line gives new inspiration for an illustration. When you possibly have any new ideas in your mind please let me know, as I can always make alterations. I would be greatly pleased if my collaboration would contribute to the success of your book

Enid admitted to David White that it was the first time she was prepared to let an illustrator work with such little guidance from her, since Harmsen instinctively understood her vision for the exact look of every page:

> I have written them with a view to giving van der Beek all the scope possible for his particular genius. He'll really enjoy himself! I don't want to tell him how to interpret anything because he'll do it much better if he has a perfectly free hand. The specific titles (which will all be different of course) will each contain the name Noddy. In the end, if they are very successful, they'll probably be referred to and ordered as the Noddy books. What do you think about it?

What White thought is that he had struck gold, and when the finished pages with their brightly coloured artwork landed on his desk a few weeks later, the overall appearance of Enid's latest brainchild far surpassed all his expectations. Enid was equally thrilled with the first images she saw too, and gathered the whole household to admire them the day they were delivered to Green Hedges. Noddy was her passion project, and soon became her sole priority. Everybody agreed that the warm and simple drawings were indeed something special, but nobody could have predicted the frenzy when the first story hit the shelves. *Noddy Goes To Toyland*, published in 1949, was an unprecedented sensation and the most successful creation of Enid's career, smashing all her previous sales records. The year 1951 marked the peak of her production, publishing thirty-seven titles that year alone. Some critics suggested Enid's sudden surge in popularity was a passing fad, and it would soon pass. How wrong they were. Blyton mania exploded, and even though Noddy was typical of all Enid's previous stories, full of humour, adventure, morals and a happy ending, the cheerful little chap from Toyland bought her fame and fortune beyond her wildest dreams. Her name became known across the globe as little Noddy took on an almost cult-like status.

For the first time Enid was described as a 'phenomenon', by Eileen Colwell, the Children's Librarian at Hendon in North London. And in *20ʰ Century Children's Books*, author Frank Eyre wrote: 'The innumerable and invariably successful contributions of Enid Blyton to this field must also be noted – they are a phenomenon.' Many others who had been dismissive in the past were coming round to the idea that Enid's contribution to children's literature was something to be applauded. Critic Wallace Hildick commented that the stories could bring great satisfaction and pleasure to many children, regardless of their ability. He said:

> A child of limited intelligence, who has nevertheless learned to read with reasonable fluency will derive great pleasure from a Blyton book's mechanical easiness alone; while a child of higher intelligence – to whom that form of easiness is irrelevant – will derive great pleasure from using it as an efficient screen on which to project fantasies of his own. (And for the former type of child there is then the added bonus of being able to read and enjoy a book which a more gifted school friend also enjoys).

Sales soared beyond even the most optimistic expectations, and Enid's publishers had trouble meeting the phenomenal demands of bookshops for fresh stock. They were selling out almost as soon as new deliveries arrived. Children around the world were charmed by the cheeky little woodland creature who meant well but always seemed to land himself in trouble, and needed to be helped by his toy friends. Enid had been right to put her faith in Van Der Beek, as children everywhere adored his distinctive drawings. The public appetite for more and more Noddy stories was immense, and to satisfy the daily demand between books, Enid landed a lucrative contract to provide a daily comic strip for the *London Evening Standard*, also to be illustrated by Van Der Beek. Enid accepted the challenge with her usual confidence, but the immense pressure and tight deadlines of a daily news-paper quickly proved too much for the artist. Van Der Beek found himself having to work late into the night and admitted that he was occasionally hal-lucinating, seeing visions of little Noddies that would appear from nowhere and crawl all over his desk. Harmsen died in Holland in 1953, just four years after the series began, but left such an enormous body of work that Enid could carry on producing books until she could no longer physically write at all. Harmsen's great legacy was that his work still lives on today through many other artists who were able to copy his work effectively after his death thanks to a special Noddy dictionary which the publishers created giving detailed descriptions of every character and a map of Toyland.

It was clear from the start that Noddy was going to be so much more than simply a series of books. As marketing experts and toy manufacturers realised the potential selling power of Enid's latest creation, they quickly swooped in and started bombarding her with suggestions for merchandising opportunities. Within months High Street shops were packed with a vast range of Noddy products, including dozens of soft toys, games and puzzles, as well as clothing, stationery, sweets, pottery and furnishings. At Christmas the market exploded with yet more collectible models of the characters, special editions of the books and specially themed games and festive decorations. It was all new to Enid who was fascinated by the marketing ideas that were being presented to her and oversaw all the merchandise just as meticulously as she would check the drawings for her books. Nothing was left to chance. She had a business acumen and pragmatic attitude to making money that was way ahead of her time, and it was certainly highly unusual for women to be leading tough financial negotiations in an almost untested market, but Enid knew what she wanted and would let nothing and nobody stand in her way. Noddy may have led to the most vicious criticism she had ever faced, but his creation was a stroke of sheer ingenuity which was not equalled for many years.

By the end of the 1950s more than 20 million copies of Noddy books had been sold in England alone. It was Enid's greatest triumph in terms of sheer volume. Throughout the decade she continued to be swamped with requests from artistic companies wanting to dramatise the stories into children's plays and pantomimes, although she resisted until she had time to write a proper script. When she asked her agent George Greenfield if he thought it was a good idea, he replied: 'I reckon that if you put your mind to it, you could write pretty well anything.' Two weeks later the finished script of *Noddy In Toyland* was in his hands. The play was 2½ hours long and included thirty-three songs. It was performed for the first time over Christmas 1954 at the Stoll Theatre in London, to sell-out audiences. Children were enraptured by seeing Toyland come to life before their eyes and the theatre was packed night after night. Enid was delighted and took all her associates to see it, as well as the children, although they were both grown up by then. She had taken a great interest in every detail of the production, and wished only that her friend Harmsen had been there to see his vision brought to life. It is still considered one of the most successful shows ever created for children. The show would go on to be produced every season for many years, not only in the capital but in provincial theatres and around the world too.

Noddy was hot property, and became a familiar household name as Enid's stories were transformed into more scripts for stage productions and television series. Enid, always intrigued by new forms of media and the opportunities they presented, wanted her stories to play a major part when she heard that Britain's first commercial television channel was due to be launched. To her delight she was soon contacted by Norman Collins, one of the directors of ATV, as the new channel was to be known. He asked her to help select the puppets to appear in a series he had planned, and as she tended to do with all new projects, Enid wanted to be heavily involved in the production. She found the whole process great fun, and was even happy to lie down on the floor of Collins' central London office to see exactly what the puppets would look like from below. A film was made of the pantomime too. But while it was another smash hit, breaking all box office records during its first season, Enid later made a very rare admission – that she had actually experienced some difficulty when it came to writing the film script. For the first time, the words did not flow freely from her imagination and she found the process challenging. Enid explained in one of her letters to psychologist Peter McKellar that her usual method of visualising the stories on a cinema screen in her mind had proved to be 'a complete failure' when she was writing for a real cinema screen:

> It was very odd. I stumbled over the writing. I laboured, I could not draw on my imagination at all. Then like a flash I seemed to discard the old way of writing, and instead of needing to see the characters in their story setting and using the 'cinema screen', into my mind came the stage itself. And then in came the characters on this stage, singing, talking, dancing – and once again something went 'click' and the whole process of writing the play went out of my hands and was taken over by my imagination again. I no longer stumbled, puzzled, tried to invent.

And although Enid had never tackled writing music to accompany her song lyrics before, she also rose to that challenge with her usual flair, and revealed that she had already thought of exactly the same tunes as the musical director Philip Green before he suggested them to her: 'Although I did not tell him – I was afraid he would think me unduly conceited,' she confided to McKellar. As well as grasping the demands of the musical score, Enid was equally in synch with the production's expert set designer Richard Lake, whom she described as 'quite a genius' and was delighted that he also seemed to be able to perfectly execute her precise visions of how Toyland should look. She said: 'He managed to produce designs that exactly fitted my own visualised conceptions, in particular some dungeon scenes – which I had not even explained to him in detail. I was amazed when I saw them and could not keep from exclaiming. It was almost as if he had seen into my mind and drawn what was there.' Enid had never met theatrical people before and was most amused by them and the way they worked. Her trips to central London grew more frequent during this time. Buoyed by the triumph of *Noddy In Toyland*, Enid was eager to produce more plays and quickly followed it up with several more scripts, but none of them really achieved the same level of success. The character of Noddy meanwhile was more popular than ever, as thousands of children named their pets after him and his best friend Big Ears. Mr Plod entered the language as it became a commonly used nickname for British policemen.

Enid was basking in the success of her life, and truly believed that all she was doing was providing young children with exciting stories, and so she was completely unprepared for the viciousness of the backlash when it came. One of the early signs of the sneering that was to follow was Geoffrey Trease's analysis of children's literature, *Tales Out of School*. He commented: 'The Blyton school stories entertain but can hardly be said to go far in depicting reality stimulating the imagination or educating the emotions. Their style is drained of all difficulty until it achieves a kind of aesthetic anaemia.' His highly influential book placed great emphasis on the need for children's literature to represent reality, not whimsy frivolity or fantasy. He disapproved of gangs of children outwitting bumbling grown-ups, flying chairs or animals that could speak.

Enid was utterly baffled when parents and educational experts began to question her moral codes and she faced damning accusations of racism that would forever tarnish her glittering career. Perhaps she had been naïve in believing that everyone would merely accept her stories as innocent fuel for children's fantasies with question or analysis. Unfortunately adults reading the books to their children did not share her young readers' unconditional admiration. Many started to feel that Enid's leading characters, who were usually from the same white and middle-class background as Enid herself, showed vindictive or cruel behaviour towards others who were of different social or ethnic background. Some questioned the nature of Noddy's close relationship with Big Ears, since they tended to share a bed, implying there may have been undertones of a homosexual relationship between the characters. In *Hurrah for Little Noddy*, Enid wrote: 'They squashed into Big Ears' tiny, soft bed, put their arms round one another to stop themselves from rolling out, and fell fast asleep.'

The frequent use of corporal punishment generally, and 'a good spanking' specifically, was also criticised but the most widespread condemnation that Enid endured was racial discrimination and stereotyping as she used gypsies and black golliwog dolls as villains in several of the stories. In *Here Comes Noddy Again* golliwogs lured Noddy into the Dark Wood where they stole his car and clothes. She wrote:

> It was the golliwog. He was so black that Noddy couldn't see him, and bumped into him when he walked out to find him. Three black faces suddenly appeared in the light of the car's lamps, and three golliwogs came running to the car. In a trice they had hold of poor Noddy and pulled him right out of his little car.

They were captured in a sack: 'The policeman drove off with the sack of squealing, squirming golliwogs,' she concluded.

In another story with the controversial title *The Three Golliwogs* the characters were named Golly, Woggie and Nigger, and she wrote: 'He would have gone red if his face hadn't have been black.' There was confusion in the story because all three appeared so similar to Mr Fussy:

> He saw a golly on the ground. He saw another on one side of him, and a third on the other – and they all looked exactly alike! 'It's a bad dream!' he shouted. 'One golly has turned into three! Help! Help! Help!' Poor Mr Fussy! He always runs away when he sees a golliwog now – and really I'm not surprised.

In *The Little Black Doll*, Enid described a toy called Sambo as having 'tight curly black hair and a smile that showed his very white teeth'. When he asked the other toys in the nursery why they did not like him, the reply from the big teddy bear was: 'Well, you see, you're black. Dolls aren't supposed to be black. You look queer to us.' Sambo was scorned until rainwater 'washes away his ugly black face'. He reappeared pink, and said: 'Now perhaps you won't dislike me because I am black.'

No matter how popular the books were with children, their parents were starting to resist and Noddy found himself under the most fire throughout most of the 1950s and 1960s. Enid was accused of blatant xenophobia, and criticised for portraying many of her working class characters as criminals. One librarian even went as far as calling Enid a neo-fascist. Enid argued that there were far more good golliwogs in her tales than bad ones, and the real villains were far more likely to be teddies, monkeys or goblins. She insisted: 'Golliwogs are merely lovable black toys, not Negroes. Teddy bears are also toys, but if there happens to be a naughty one in my books for younger children, this does not mean that I hate bears!' Her own children were given black dolls to play with, although they later felt that Enid had passed her own feelings on to them, and Imogen gave away her doll which was wearing a nurse's uniform: 'I knew no black people and I found the uniform somewhat alarming,' she said. 'Perhaps it was an early distaste for my own feelings of xenophobia.'

Without question the terminology Enid used is completely unacceptable today, although she appeared to have no idea that her characters might be deemed controversial. She believed she was reflecting attitudes, albeit unfortunate ones, which were commonplace at the time; and as such her work should be placed in that context. She did not invent the idea of golliwogs, they were based on real minstrel dolls that children would apparently pelt with rubber balls for being ugly, and they had been adapted into characters by previous children's authors. The term was derived from the fifteenth-century word polliwog, used to describe a tadpole which had black flesh. Golliwogs had first appeared in a children's story by an English writer and artist called Florence Kate Upton in 1895, when she was just 22-years-old. Having studied as an artist in New York, she returned to England in the hope of raising money for further tuition after her father died. She was staying with an aunt in Hampstead, north London, and after discovering an old black-faced rag doll in the attic, she was inspired to write a children's story about it. Upton said later: 'As the golliwog has always seemed to me to be telling me his own biography, so in the same way he must have told me his own name. I picked him up from the table in my studio, and without intention of naming him, without the idea of a name passing through my mind, I called him Golliwogg.'

At the time the name had no negative connotations, and Florence enlisted the help of her mother Bertha to write the words to go with her illustrations. Their first book *The Adventures of Two Dutch Dolls and a Golliwogg* was completed in 1894 and published the following year. In the story, the golliwog, dressed in red trousers with a white shirt and blue coat was initially described as 'a horrid sight, the blackest gnome', but turned out later to be good, loveable and brave, with a 'kind face'. The book proved an instant hit with the British public, and after sales spread across Europe and to America and Australia, Florence and her mother Bertha went on to produce a whole series of golliwog adventures. Twelve more books were published over the next fourteen years, with tales of the golliwog toy having various adventures all around the world with his friends the Dutch Dolls, called Peg and Sarah Jane.

After that, in 1899, author Helen Bannerman wrote *The Story of Little Black Sambo*, in which his family were described as 'irresponsible plantation niggers'. Bannerman, who was born in Edinburgh, married an army doctor and lived with him in Madras, India, where she wrote the story about a clownish but greedy little boy. And a contemporary of Enid's, author Captain W.E. Johns, created jingoistic fighter pilot Captain James Biggles in 1932 and in one of the books a character talks about 'Indians, niggers, and half-breeds, the scum of the earth.' The brave hero spent much of his time in combat with the German enemy, and while the original books may now be looked back upon with incredulity, at the time they were almost as popular as Enid's stories.

Meanwhile, the term 'wog' had started to be used as a derogatory racial slur for black people. First popularised during the Second World War, it was uttered by some British soldiers to insult North Africans and other foreigners, and its meaning spread to include anybody with even slightly dark skin. Its origin has been hotly disputed – the acronym for the term Wily Oriental Gentleman is one suggested derivation, but it is more likely that it was adapted from the much better known golliwog. When Enid was writing, and indeed buying toys for her own children, a number of toy companies were producing black-faced dolls. Slightly changing the name by dropping the second G, they released a flurry of toys and badges on to the market which were coveted by children until the late twentieth century. The largest producer was the German company Steiff, whose original golliwog dolls went on sale in 1908. In 1910, John Robertson of the jam-manufacturing family business James Robertson & Sons saw some children playing with one of these dolls and decided to make one the company's mascot. Golly first appeared on the Paisley firm's jam jars that year, and in the 1920s the company began producing Golliwog badges and enamel brooches which could be claimed by collecting tokens from labels. Featuring golliwogs playing various sporting activities, the badges remained sought after for decades, and spawned other toys, watches and even dinner sets which became a part of everyday life.

But when the characters were increasingly used with negative connotations, and the term became an unacceptable slur, they became much more contentious figures. Enid was seen as one of the worst culprits of racial stereotyping, having repeatedly portrayed golliwogs as naughty thieves. By the 1960s, both the use of the term and the dolls themselves were under attack, and have now all but disappeared. In 1983 the Greater London Council deemed Robertson's products offensive and banned them from its jurisdiction. By 1988 the character could no longer be used in TV advertising. After holding out for many years, the Robertson firm was forced to jettison Golly entirely in 2002: 'We sell 45 million jars of jam and marmalade each year and they have pretty much all got Golly on them,' said a spokesperson for the company. 'He's still very popular. Each year we get more than 340,000 requests for Golly badges. Since 1910 we have sent out more than 20 million.'

But Enid was writing at a time of different values and claimed to not understand the sensitivity surrounding the issue, since she meant no harm. Being accused of racism was baffling enough to her, but she was far more hurt by the suggestion that she had not actually written all the stories herself. Since she was dealing with no less than twelve different publishing houses many people became convinced by the persistent rumour that Enid had reached the stage where she just put her famous signature to work produced by a team of writers. At one stage she was churning out up to 10,000 words in a day and could produce a *Famous Five* story in a week, leading cynics to argue that it was not physically possible for one person to produce such vast quantities of work on her own. It was hardly surprising given that she had more than thirty books published a year, but the story that she was running a factory of ghost writers somewhere churning out books on her behalf was a smear that floored Enid, particularly when she received angry letters from children accusing her of being a liar and a fraud. Some readers had even heard that Enid was already dead so various other people must be writing the books in her name. Eventually Enid, who had always worked alone with her small portable Imperial typewriter, could not take it any longer so she decided she needed take legal action in a bid to stamp out these hurtful allegations before they could spread even further. She fired off a furious letter to her solicitor Arnold Thirlby, determined to discredit the rumours which were gathering weight by the day: 'This is very damaging, not only to my books, but to me,' she wrote. 'I am such a public figure now, and well trusted, as you know, and run many clubs and society which bring in money, that I absolutely must have these rumours cleared up – for who is going to believe I am honest if I don't write my own books.'

She pursued a partially successful court case against a young librarian who had spoken at the school of one of her young readers, and told pupils that Enid only put her name to the books and did not write them all. After a long- running legal battle, the librarian eventually made a public apology to Enid at the trial, and she hoped that would be the end of the matter. However, for many years the rumours doggedly continued to swirl that no lone author could possibly produce such a huge quantity of work by herself, and the only possible explanation must be that others were paid to emulate her style. Even her own daughter Imogen admitted that Enid was working at an exceptionally fast rate: 'She seems to have become almost a machine for channelling characters into books, moulding them into shape with a professional skill that was unequalled by any other children's writer,' she said.

Enid was also stung, but to a lesser degree, by the idea that she had such a limited vocabulary that her books were far too easy for most children to bother with. Enid did not like hearing any of it, but she was tough and claimed not to care. She insisted that she was not interested in what any critics over the age of 12 had to say, she understood children's secrets, how they liked to read and the fantasy worlds they liked to escape to. Her sales figures spoke for themselves, and made it hard to argue that her books were only read by a minority. When pressed on the matter she slammed her detractors as: 'Stupid people who don't know what they're talking about because they've never read any of my books.' She also maintained that the simple structure of her stories boosted the confidence of reluctant readers, and she continued to produce at least twelve new books each year. But the tide was slowly turning against her and in 1958 *Encounter* magazine dedicated an entire five pages to slating Enid and her latest creation. In a lengthy article entitled 'Dear Little Noddy – A Parent's Lament', journalist Colin Welch wrote:

> It is the most unpleasant child that he most resembles. He always had to have somebody to run to, to whine and wail at, and the machinery of benevolent authority (Big Ears) or the state (Mr Plod) could always be invoked to redress the balance between cowardice, weakness and inanity on the one hand, and vigour, strength and resource on the other.

Welch went further still, slamming Noddy as: 'An unnaturally priggish, sanctimonious, witless, spiritless, snivelling, sneaking doll,' and complained that the stories were forced on adults. He even went on to attack Enid's style:

> By writing ruthlessly down to children, she does not merely bore and antagonise grown-ups. Her *Noddy* books also fail to stretch

the imagination of children, to enlarge their experience, to kindle wonder in them or awaken their delight in words. They contain nothing incomprehensible even to the dimmest child, nothing mysterious or stimulating. By putting everything within reach of the child's mind they enervate and cripple it.

While Enid saw Noddy as a children's version of Charlie Chaplin, according to Welch he was more like the bungling comedian Norman Wisdom, and his incessant nodding of the head was a sign that perhaps he had something physically wrong: 'The clinical explanation of this palsy or St Vitus's dance is that the victim's head is supported by a spring. Yet, in the light of Noddy's manifest feeble-mindedness, it is bound to acquire a deeper and more sinister significance.' He even said that Noddy's timidity 'borders on the pathological', adding that he was 'querulous, irritable and humourless'. His piece concluded: 'In this witless, spiritless, snivelling, sneaking doll the children of England are expected to find themselves reflected.'

It was by far the most acidic attack Enid had endured and to her horror, the article went down well and started to gain traction with many other parents who believed that their children should not waste their time with Blyton books either. Librarians began to remove her books from shelves as they feared children could potentially read nothing else between the ages of 3 and 12. With paper rationing a thing of the past, and an economic upswing sweeping the nation, the supply of children's books was starting to improve hugely and librarians, who had previously found themselves swamped with almost nothing but Enid's stories, found they were at last in a position to cut back. The activities of a protest group called Librarians For Social Change started to gather momentum around the world too, and there was a storm of indignation that culminated in the books being banned entirely from a number of public libraries and schools in Australia and New Zealand. A *Daily Mail* report explained: 'Many, maybe most, of the public libraries in this country as well as Australia and New Zealand do not stock her books. Some have openly banned them. Others tacitly do not buy them.' Another piece in *New Society* added: 'The bookworms are creeping out of the woodwork – in the shape of a new group of librarians who want to actively influence library users by their selection and promotion of materials. Their predecessors, who refused to stock Enid Blyton, would applaud the principle, if not the practice.' Ruth Inglis wrote in her book *A Time To Learn*: 'British librarians have certainly decided that children can live without Enid Blyton.' And the Library Association slammed Enid's books because they were deemed to have 'mediocre plots', 'weak characterisations' and 'unimaginative' use of language. But the ban had the opposite effect when children found they were unable to borrow Enid's books from libraries – they went out and bought them instead, leading to another spike in sales. Yet there was nothing Enid could do to stop the condemnation which was by now coming at her thick and fast.

Chapter Fifteen

Enid was now a target for anyone wanting to complain about declining standards in children's literacy. There was a spate of spoof stories parodying Noddy in the newspapers, which Enid found particularly irritating, although she did manage to brush off the laughable suggestion that it was actually possible for children to become physically addicted to Blyton books, and as a result would never go on to read adult literature.

Enid felt she was chiefly concerned with the education and welfare of children, and as such she should be above this sort of criticism. When the press continued to report that the quality of her books had slumped, and she was swamping the market with poorer quality work than ever, she became very defensive. Kenneth was equally furious on her behalf and backed her in every fight since he could never see any problem – only the profits pouring into their bulging bank accounts. But Enid was consoled by the fact that hundreds of thousands of children continued to clamour as loudly as ever for more and more books. Children were certainly not complaining, and they were her audience, not the high-brow literary critics who accused her of being shallow and repetitive, and it was the children who mattered to Enid more than anything else. Enid tried not to let any of the negativity that swirled around her slow her down, and continued to reach her usual quota of books and articles, made as many public appearances as ever, while closely supervising the production of *Noddy* television shows and theatrical performances.

However a report in the *Guardian* newspaper about the Library Association's centenary exhibition, held in Nottingham in November 1977, felt there might be a slight thawing towards Enid. The headline read 'Noddy and co. come in from the cold' and the article went on: 'Enid Blyton, the children's author whose work was banned by many librarians from the 1950's onwards, was rehabilitated yesterday at the opening of a major centennial exhibition of children's literature by the Library Association.' While Enid's books had been gradually phased out by some libraries, it was by no means a blanket ban across the country. The more commercially minded bookshops decided they would be doing their customers a disservice by being anti-Blyton since readers insisted they not only provided escapist pleasure for children but also encouraged an early enthusiasm for reading. Regardless of adult disapproval, in the post-war economic boom of the 1950s, children had more pocket money to buy books themselves, and most wanted to keep their own copies for their rapidly expanding collections, rather than borrow them temporarily from libraries.

Towards the end of the 1950s there was also a change of heart at the BBC. Having never used any of Enid's work despite repeated requests by her and Kenneth, there was a special programme made about her career which was included in a series called *Success Stories*, and her book *The Island of Adventure* was featured in a week of *Jackanory* children's programmes. But Enid was by no means accepted by the establishment, and the mockery continued. And so in 1951, at the peak of the Noddy frenzy, Enid decided to change tack completely and wrote a much more serious novel. *The Six Bad Boys* tackled the troubled lives of a group of anti-social children who all came from vastly different economic backgrounds. In the story three of the children from the Berkeley family were abandoned by their father following a string of arguments between him and their mother – who then took great pains to conceal his unexpected disappearance.

It had been more than forty years since Enid's father had left home, but the scars had not healed, and she described the painful experience vividly in *The Six Bad Boys*. The young characters in the story were glad of their schoolwork to distract them from what was going on behind closed doors at home, just as Enid and her siblings had been. Enid's brother Hanly was extremely moved when he came to read the story for the first time and confirmed that, apart from changing the gender of the three children involved, it was an accurate portrayal of precisely what had happened to the Blyton family during that traumatic time. Describing the moment Mr and Mrs Berkeley split up, Enid wrote:

> The children were huddled together on the top stairs, listening .
> . . shivering . . . partly with cold, partly with fear. Those dreadful
> rows! They all put their arms round one another for warmth. Their
> father spoke in a quiet voice. 'This is the end. It's not good for any
> of us to go on like this. I am sure that you are right when you say
> that I am to blame for everything. So I'm going. Then perhaps you
> will be happier, all of you.'
> The front door slammed. The front gate clicked shut. Quick
> footsteps went down the lane, and then faded away. He did not

come back. That was a dreadful time for the three children. They had to cope with a tearful angry mother. They had to promise her not to tell anyone their father had gone away because of a row. They had to say he was gone on a visit. They had to face the fact that perhaps their father might never come back again.

And, just as in Enid's own childhood, the fictitious neighbours were unsympathetic towards Mrs Berkeley since they felt her poor husband had done nothing wrong. A character called Mrs Mackenzie echoed young Enid herself when she said:

> 'There are always faults on both sides, and your biggest fault, both of you, is that you only think of yourselves and not of the children. Poor things, going about with anxious looks, pretending their father's on a visit! Can't you see what you're doing to those children of yours? You write to that husband of yours and tell him you're missing him and the children are too; tell him you'll turn over a new leaf for their sake, if only he'd come back.'

When their children ended up in court, the parents were blamed for their wrongdoing just as much as the culprits themselves. They were reprimanded by the magistrate and the children were sent to live with foster families in the countryside, since their working mother was deemed unfit to take adequate care of them. Enid wrote: 'He had the reports about Bob's mother before him – and many a time before he had similar reports of children going wrong because their mothers had left them in order to go out to work.' Writing about disadvantaged children and social upheaval in this way was a major departure for Enid, until this point almost all her families were cheerful and fun-loving, and the parents tended to stay well out of the children's way. Although she included two middle-class boys, they were equally unhappy characters. Prior to this Enid had never really written in any sort of serious detail about the effects a broken home could have on a child, and it was a surprising change of direction. These troublesome boys came home to empty houses, and were 'spanked' and 'whacked' by their fathers. The story ended happily, but *The Six Bad Boys* painted a simplistic view of working women and single parents. Enid's attitude towards traditional male and female roles in the home left her open to yet more accusations of sexism and gender stereotyping. Her views of family models and physical punishments seem out-dated today, but they were more commonly held at the time. While Enid herself worked long hours of course, and left much of her own children's care to boarding schools and nannies, she did her writing in the home.

She worked closely on the project with Basil Henriques, a juvenile court chairman who helped explain to her how children deemed by society as bad were just the same as the well-behaved ones in many ways. Enid was fascinated by all he had to teach her and had a great deal of respect for Henriques' work. He wrote a foreword in the first edition in 1951 praising it for the way it showed how six different boys could get into serious trouble for very different reasons. Henriques explained:

> It is generally admitted that the 'broken home' is one of the main causes of children getting into trouble. It is the unhappy children rather than the 'bad' ones who come before the courts, and it is the broken home which so often causes unhappiness in children, especially when the phrase is interpreted to include the home in which the parents quarrel in front of the children, and from which the mother goes out to work at times when she is needed by them.

He added that the way Enid had described the workings of the minds of the children Bob Kent and Tom Berkeley was 'absolutely brilliant', saying: 'It shows why the broken home causes children to go wrong, and the gradual deterioration of both boys is told in a manner which I have never seen surpassed.'

In the book, the character of Bob compares his working mother unfavourably with Mrs Mackenzie, the stay at home mother of his twin friends: 'The twins mother was always so kind, Bob thought. She always seemed pleased to see them whenever they came back from school. She didn't mind hugging them when they hugged her. He was quite sure they never seemed to bother her. She was a real mother.' In her preface, Enid wrote that she had created the story not simply to entertain but also 'to explain some of the wrong things there are in the world, and to help put them right'. She added:

> I love children, good or bad. I know plenty of good ones – and I have been to the Juvenile Courts and seen plenty of bad ones. One of the finest magistrates of these Courts is the well-known Mr Basil Henriques, who deals so wisely and kindly with all the delinquent children brought before him. I have watched him at his court dealing with these children.

Although the book was well received by literary critics, perhaps because it was clear more effort and certainly a great deal more research had gone into it than any of Enid's previous books, it was not as popular with children. She had one further attempt at social commentary with *The Family At Red Roofs*, about the Jackson children who struggled to survive after their father went abroad on business and his ship was wrecked. While he was apparently drowned, their mother was taken gravely ill. But they triumphed over various disasters and eventually their father returned. Both these stories were attempts by Enid at capturing the gritty social realism of the time. She certainly explored the anger she still felt about her father leaving decades earlier, but since she had always been so reluctant to discuss what really happened at the time, hardly anybody guessed she was writing from personal experience.

Enid was often accused of being out of touch with the real world, but another issue she felt passionately about was the abolition of capital punishment for child murderers. During an incendiary parliamentary debate on the subject in 1950, Enid wrote a surprisingly gritty poem entitled 'To Hang or Not To Hang – that is the Question! Two Points of View'. The final verse was:

> And you ask me WHY I would hang this man!
> Though you know it's our only hope
> To stop any fiend who would rape and kill –
> He's a coward – and he fears the rope!
> You're not quite sure if I'm right or not?
> You'll think about it – alone?
> Well, if you're doubtful, I'm certain of this –
> You haven't a child of your own!

These views almost never made it into Enid's writing for children, where there was no place for violence, rape or torture. In 1957 she attempted her first adult play, *The Summer Storm*, but only too aware of the public bias against her at the time, Enid decided to use a fake name, Justin Geste, in the hope of avoiding any adverse comment influencing how the production was received. The idea of writing for adults meant a great deal to her, and she was uncharacteristically nervous as she sent her manuscript to a number of theatrical agents and managers. Unfortunately, the pseudonym made no difference and the overly dramatic storyline about marital intrigue was deemed unsuitable and unfashionable at a time when the infamous Angry Young Men were starting to fill theatres. Enid's play, which was set in an upper middle-class family, was the complete opposite of what audiences wanted, but she had not realised how much tastes had changed. She and Kenneth rarely went to the theatre since his deafness meant he could never really enjoy plays, and she seemed unable to develop adult characters convincingly, and the script never reached the stage. Enid was wounded by the lack of enthusiasm for her latest project, and when she was advised to rewrite the play, she simply refused. She was down but not out, and surrounded herself once again with children whom she knew would never dream of hurting her feelings.

Enid did not need to bother with anyone who might criticise her, she was well established as a hugely famous star in the world of children's literature, and she had never been in greater demand to make public appearances across the country. There were scores of invitations to lavish parties and functions, and constant requests for her to make charity appeals. She even received an invitation to a royal garden party at Buckingham Palace but did not like the crowds or the endless waiting around so she declined the following year and was never invited again. Enid was most flattered when she was asked to read her stories to schools or to sign copies of the books. She enjoyed lengthy autograph-signing sessions at her favourite bookstores which included Blackwell's in Oxford, as she had struck up a friendship with the owner Basil Blackwell, and of course Harrods in London where she always received a warm welcome since she was such a valued and loyal customer. Every appearance drew enormous crowds of highly excited children who would often become very rowdy waiting for Enid to arrive. But the moment she stood up and calmly said 'Hallo children' they would immediately fall silent and settle down happily to hear her tell a story. Within minutes they were gripped. Her air of authority and clear voice meant she could manage to keep complete control, no matter how large or unruly the audience was.

There was no let-up in the demand for her books either, and when cheap paperback versions of the Noddy stories came out at the start of the 1960s, and there was another sharp spike in sales. Every time a child wrote to her begging for one more book, she could not resist. Imogen was away at university and Gillian, who had graduated with a history degree from St Andrew's University in Scotland, was living in the US, so the timing could not have been better for Enid to retire. She considered it for Kenneth's sake, he was worried about her health, but he also knew how miserable she would be without her work to keep her busy, and how stubborn she was.

Enid's relationship with her daughters had thawed slightly when Imogen had followed in her older sister's footsteps and gone to study at

St Andrew's, after reluctantly completing a domestic science course at her mother's insistence. But Enid still had the power to sting with her icy words. Imogen was particularly hurt when her first boyfriend, a student at Cambridge named Peter, invited her to the May Ball and Enid did not hide her disapproval. Imogen said: 'I became aware that she was listening in to my telephone conversations. I overheard her saying to my stepfather – and I was meant to overhear – "Imogen thinks of nothing but boys now. Don't you think it is disgusting Kenneth?" He deserved better of any girlfriend's mother.' Enid and Kenneth only visited Imogen at St Andrew's once during the four years she was a student there, to attend her graduation ceremony, but she would have preferred them not to bother to making the journey: 'It was an uncomfortable experience for all of us and I would much rather have graduated on my own,' she said.

Enid did not want to admit it, but her health was slowly beginning to deteriorate. She had never been a woman who would do anything against her will, but she was unable to sleep or focus properly, and this time she did not have a choice but to ease up on work. In May 1957 she was taken ill during a round of golf with Kenneth at their local club in Beaconsfield. She complained that she was feeling breathless and faint, so Kenneth insisted she go home for a rest and immediately called one of his doctor friends from London, a heart specialist. Haunted by her father's unexpected fatal heart attack years earlier, Enid was frantic with worry and feared the worst. When the cardiologist arrived and examined his very agitated patient, he managed to console her by saying that it was not a heart attack causing her pain as she had feared, in fact she had developed a digestive malfunction from being hunched over her typewriter for so many hours at a time. She refused to believe the cardiologist and became so anxious that he prescribed her sedatives. The specialist reassured Enid that she was fine to continue working, but when her daughters returned home for a visit a few weeks later, Kenneth told them that their mother had actually had a heart attack. He told them that Enid needed to drastically cut down her work load and not take on anything that might cause her any strain or stress. Why Kenneth would choose to conceal or ignore his friend's expert diagnosis is unclear, perhaps he hoped she would retire, but he had also been worried for quite some time about her mental health breaking down too. He had begun to notice that her memory was beginning to fail and Kenneth was doing his best to cover up various lapses on his wife's behalf. It was certainly in his own interests for her to ease up on work, but Enid reminded him that she had always been remarkably healthy apart from a bout of pneumonia and a time she was badly bitten on the leg by a dog which led to a short stay in hospital.

But this time she was rattled and agreed to take a break from work, in any case the prescribed sedatives forced her to take long rests. Regardless of her wish to keep her illness quiet, news did get out and Enid was inundated with letters and cards from fans wishing her a speedy recovery. She had no choice but to address the matter and wrote in the *Enid Blyton Magazine*:

> I know that a great many of you learnt that I had been ill, because I had so many anxious letters from you wishing me well again! Some of you reproached me for not letting you know about it in my magazine letter – and perhaps I ought to have told you instead of risking your hearing about it suddenly from the newspapers. But I did not want to worry you, as I was sure I would soon get better. I had been working much too hard – but as you know, I do so love my work for you children and there was so much to do this year! I shall be sensible in future and not work so hard, but it is going to be very, very difficult.

She said work would take a back seat, but that proved an impossible promise for Enid to keep, and before long her diary was packed again. Although she had cut down on the amount of writing she agreed to, instead she allowed herself to get swept up in the planning of another *Noddy In Toyland* production. Kenneth did his best to make sure she took rests between commitments, and they were both forced to reduce their more strenuous activities such as their regular golf games since she still suffered from breathlessness from time to time, and his arthritis was getting worse. By the time he retired from St Stephen's Hospital in 1957, at the age of 65, the pain was so bad that he would have to be propped up by a stool in order to operate on his patients. He put the arthritis down to a mild bout of poliomyelitis which he had suffered in 1947, and believed he had contracted it from Imogen and openly blamed her for it: 'My defences shielded me from the pain and my reason told me that I could not in any way be blamed,' Imogen wrote later.

Kenneth had looked forward to a happy retirement, but that was not to be. He was often in agony and hated not being allowed to do as he pleased. He had to give up tennis and the couple started to use an electric caddy car to drive them around the golf course in order to still play occasionally. After a while golf became impossible too and he could no longer visit his beloved Studland, and was forced to take up stamp collecting instead, spending many evenings building up what would eventually become a large and valuable collection. He longed to move abroad, as he was convinced that a warmer climate would be good for his poor health, but that plan did not suit Enid who refused to leave her treasured garden at Green Hedges, and insisted that she still needed to be close to her publishers. She tried to focus on getting herself well again, especially as Gillian had announced she was getting married in August to a television producer called Donald Baverstock. Enid was thrilled and wanted Gillian to have the perfect wedding, which she always felt she had been denied herself. But Enid was not well enough to oversee the arrangements – which included a ceremony at St James' in Piccadilly followed by a lavish reception at the Savoy Hotel in London. The exclusive hotel had become a regular haunt of Enid's, and she chose it for most of her business lunches and threw Imogen's 21st birthday party there too.

Unable to help with the arrangements for Gillian's wedding, she left Kenneth to finalise the plans and took herself off to Swanage for a rest, in the hope that she might be refreshed for the big day. But when Kenneth joined her at their holiday home, he was shocked by how unwell she seemed and wanted to postpone the wedding. A couple of days later however, Kenneth called Gillian and told her to go ahead as planned since her mother was feeling much better and would be able to travel back to London in time. Many guests noticed how tired and uncomfortable Enid was looking during the service and she appeared strained at the reception, but she did not want anyone to know that she had been ill again.

While Kenneth's ailments manifested themselves physically, Enid became better at hiding her mental impairments, and refused to admit to anybody how bad it was getting since her greatest fear had always been losing her brilliant photographic memory. Throughout her life she had always relied heavily on the 'card index' function of her brain, but now it was starting to fail her and she was terrified of losing control. She wrote to Peter McKellar: 'I dread the feeling of losing my identity of not being able to control my own mind!'

She started to forget names of people and everyday objects. She and Kenneth tried to help each other out and cover for one another as much as they could. She did not want anyone to know that her memory was failing her, and did her best to maintain as many public appearances and readings as she could, but she was easily distracted and it frightened Kenneth. As a medical student many years earlier he had seen mental patients in the Bethlem Asylum and feared mental illness more than any other disease. He tried to take as much of the stress of Enid's business affairs away as possible, but soon she was incapable of doing much to help him. She found it harder and harder to meet her husband's needs and became increasingly distressed by seeing him in such physical pain. It was a very miserable time for both of them. By the mid–1960s Enid was finding it more and more difficult to write coherently, while Kenneth's illness had got drastically worse and had led to various worrying health complications. Neither of them were prepared to admit how serious their respective situations were, and as Enid slid slowly into the grip of senile dementia they hid themselves away from the outside world, covering up for each other's blunders and mishaps as best they could. Enid had always fervently prayed she would be affected physically and not mentally in her old age. But her very worst fears were coming true.

Her concentration span grew shorter, and when Enid's short and medium term memory failed her, Kenneth would deal with publishers on her behalf, and made sure he read over her letters before she sent them out. She was unable to write anything after 1963, and her final three books were published the following year.

Chapter Sixteen

When she was distracted with work, Enid could easily brush off the barrage of criticism she faced, and did not spend time dwelling on past problems or indeed any difficult emotional issues. But now with time on her hands Enid was forced to confront some of her old demons, and she found herself brooding for hours over various unhappy events of her past. For the first time she realised she was wracked with guilt over the way she had abandoned her mother and brothers.

During this time Hanly contacted her to say their mother was gravely ill, and longed to see her before it was too late. Theresa had repeatedly begged Enid to visit over the years, but she had always refused, and even when she knew her mother lay dying in hospital in Maidstone she would not make any attempt at a reconciliation. Gillian and Imogen had never met their grandmother and nor had she been introduced to either Hugh or Kenneth. Enid told them she had been brought up by the Attenborough family after running away from home as a small child. Since their younger brother Carey was living abroad, much of Theresa's care in her old age had been left to Hanly, although he was also struggling to look after his two sick children and a bed-ridden wife. After Enid and Carey had left home many years earlier, Hanley had stayed behind out of loyalty to their mother. He was the most sensitive of the three children and took on sole responsibility for her care until the end of her life. She suffered from dementia for almost ten years but Hanly's pleas for help were unsuccessful, with Enid claiming she was too busy to come and make peace – sending money instead.

When Theresa died, Hanly urged Enid to come to the funeral, but again she insisted she was too busy. It would have been a stark reminder of the past she had blocked out many years earlier. According to Imogen, her mother was going through the menopause at the time which made her prone to irrational decisions and emotional outbursts, including one occasion when she remarked to Kenneth in front of her daughter: 'I do dislike people with inferiority complexes. Don't you think that Imogen has a dreadful inferiority complex?' If Imogen was stung by the harsh barb, she tried her best not to show it and remarked later: 'It was a good thing that my defences were, by now, adequate.'

But news of Enid's estranged mother's death had an unexpected effect. Enid found herself grieving over her father's early death which she had never really dealt with at the time, and she began to regret the brutal way she had cut Hugh out of his daughter's lives. She had broken her promise to let Hugh see them and he had long since given up fighting her over it, as Enid refused every request he made, and he could not bring himself to contest it anymore either. But Enid knew in her heart she had betrayed him by going back on her original promise, and now it was too late. It finally dawned on her that she had done to her own children what her father had done to her, and started to feel some sympathy for Theresa who she had cut off so long ago. For the first time Enid was unable to keep her mind distracted from these thoughts, and was devastated as she looked back on how she had behaved. She could not stop thinking about happy childhood memories, and was forced to admit to Kenneth that she had lied to him about the circumstances of her leaving home. It was too late to make peace with her mother, but she wished she had not coldly ignored Theresa's frequent emotionally charged pleas for a reconciliation, especially during her final years when she knew she did not have long left to live.

It was a strange time for Enid and it took a heavy toll on her mentally, she found it difficult to sleep, and felt tired, irritable and depressed. She became introspective, and examining herself for the first time, did not like what she saw. Gillian recalled her saying: 'I'm finding it so difficult to read now, because I can't remember what I've just read.' By 1966 Kenneth was virtually dictating all her correspondence, but even then her mind would wander and as she lost concentration she would make mistakes. She would write dozens of notes to remind herself of things she needed to do, although when she later discovered her own scribbles she would often have no idea what they meant. Endless scraps of paper accumulated all over the house, most of which she did not even remember writing. Enid spent hours at a time in a kind of dream world, and found it increasingly difficult to focus. She had become a grandmother by this stage, and longed for her grandchildren to visit but when they did she would drift off. Gillian and Donald had four young children and moved to Yorkshire so it was difficult for them to make the long journey often, while Imogen and her new husband Duncan Smallwood were living in Sussex.

There were of course moments of clarity, usually when someone was discussing her books or when she was reading letters from young readers who still enjoyed her stories, but she preferred painting watercolours of her garden to writing. When her recent memories completely deserted her, Enid began to live in her distant past. Her day-to-day existence was confused, muddled and disordered, and as her adult life all but disintegrated it was far easier for her to recall her early years.

Enid became obsessed with her own childhood. At one point in early 1967 she called Hanly and begged him to visit her urgently, despite the fact that he had not seen his sister in seventeen years. Kenneth had been taken back into hospital for a short period, and with the girls busy with their own young families, Enid confided to her brother that she was desperately lonely. He was alarmed and immediately rushed to Green Hedges from his home in Kent as she had demanded. But when Hanly arrived Enid had absolutely no memory of having called him in the first place. It took some time for her to even recognise him, and when she finally worked out who he was, Enid wanted him to take her back to their childhood home in Beckenham to see their parents. She had completely forgotten that both her mother and father were dead, and all she could recall were the happy times before Thomas and Theresa had split up. The bitterness and pain she had endured had been erased from her memory. Hanly was deeply disturbed by the confused and troubled state he found his estranged sister in, and continued to visit her regularly after that, and even agreed to her repeated requests to go and visit the house where they had grown up together. She was so fixated on the idea that he felt he had no choice but to relent and they returned to look at their childhood house together. He hoped that showing her that their old life no longer existed might snap Enid out of her memory loss, but it made no difference and she remained in a kind of dream world and continued to say that all she wanted was to 'go home'.

Kenneth, who had barely left her side in months, was taken to a London hospital in September 1967 and died a week later. Enid wrote simply in her diary that evening: 'My darling Kenneth died. I loved him so much. I feel lost and unhappy.' The shock of his death seemed to jolt Enid back into life briefly. She launched herself into action, busily organising his funeral and cremation in nearby Amersham, but after a few days of lucidity she relapsed again and talked of little else but her childhood home and how much she longed to go back there. She would tell visitors who came after his death: 'Kenneth won't be long. He has been playing golf you know.'

Enid had forgotten most of her adult behaviour and personality, and had become alarmingly childlike again, often behaving inappropriately and trying to run away from the house. Now in the full grip of senile dementia, although she had loathed her mother for years, she began to talk about her with great affection. She was nursed around the clock by her faithful housekeeper Doris Cox, who had been with the family since 1945, but after a while it became too much of a burden for her. Enid needed to be reminded about her illness every day, causing her great distress when she realised how helpless she was, even though it had all been explained to her the day before. Enid was moved to a nursing home in Hampstead, north London, a few months before she died on 28 November 1968, slipping away peacefully in her sleep at the age of 71. Her psychiatrist told the family that her last words had been: 'I am going to my father! At least I hope I am.'

The world Enid left behind had changed far beyond her recognition. Gone were the innocent days of sun-drenched summer picnics of boiled eggs and lashings of ginger beer, midnight feasts, lacrosse matches and camping out in hidden coves. In 1968 Robert Kennedy and Martin Luther King were assassinated, Soviet troops occupied Czechoslovakia and incidents of crime and violence were higher than ever in Britain. There was an intimate funeral held for Enid's close family and friends at Golders Green crematorium, but her memorial service at St James' Church in Piccadilly in January 1967 was packed with well-wishers including numerous staff from the various publishing houses, clubs and charities she was involved with until the end. Her eldest grandchild Sian Baverstock, who was 10-years-old at the time, read from the Bible, while one of her publishers Paul Hodder-Williams gave a glowing tribute: 'She really loved children and understood instinctively what would interest them,' he said. 'It was with children that her gift of sympathy had its greatest flowering. That is why they have loved and will continue to love the best of the books which she wrote for them and them alone.'

Enid's fans were devastated at the loss, and although Green Hedges has since been demolished, Enid's legacy lived on through her work. Many of the 750 books she produced remained in print for decades. In 1974, 6 years after her death, she was named the fourth most translated author in the world after Lenin, Marx and Jules Verne, with 149 translations having already been made in 15 different countries. Although Enid was often accused of being too English, with her stories plagued with traditional stereotypes and slang, the translations were so effective that children often remarked that they had no idea that Enid was not originally from their own country. And in some Far Eastern countries they were particularly popular because of the great desire for a British-style education.

However, the controversy surrounding the nature of Enid's work did not die with her. Critics continued to condemn her books as overly simplistic, with politically incorrect undertones that did not fit with current ways of thinking. Many years after her death, the debate raged on about the quality of her writing, although with gradually less ferocity as time passed. In the 1970s there appeared to be some nostalgia for Enid's storytelling as the demand for reality had led to some bleak and challenging children's books. They wanted a return to light-hearted storytelling and librarians were starting to face criticism for not buying her books. In 1975 *The Times Literary Supplement* wrote: 'The past fifteen years has seen a turgid wave of problem books, bombarding children with facts on abortion, menstruation, racism, mental and physical handicaps, divorce, adolescent hang ups, violence, religion and so forth. No area has remained sacred; but style, imagination and storytelling have too often been sacrificed to the golden calf of truth.'

Literary critic Aidan Chambers complained about Enid's: 'Triviality, linguistically impoverished style, anaemia in plot and characterisation, and clichéd stereotypes ideas', but later came round to accepting that there was very little adults could do to prevent her popularity among children, but questioned whether children should always get what they want. He went on to write in 1985: 'She quite literally places her second self on the side of the children in her stories and the readers she deliberately looks for. Her allegiance becomes collusion in a game of "us kids against them adults". She so allies herself with her desired readers that she fails them because she never takes them further than they are.' Describing Enid as a female Peter Pan, the boy who never grew up, Chambers said it was in her best interests for children not to grow older because that way they would stay loyal fans of hers. He wrote: 'She is the kind of suffocating adult who prefers children never to grow up, because then she can enjoy their petty foibles and dominate them by her adult superiority. This betrayal of childhood seeps through her stories; we see it as the underlying characteristic of her children who all really want to dominate each other as well as the adults.'

There was more evidence that the tide had not turned entirely, with in particular plenty of disapproval still aimed at Noddy. Particularly when critic Margery Fisher described him as 'A monstrously infantile, retarded, masochistic hero', and in her 1975 book *Who's Who In Children's Books*, she went on to say: 'He is frequently heard to say that he doesn't like being sensible but would far rather be silly, (and who) seems to have been put together from the weakest and least desirable attributes of childhood. It is hard to explain the persistent popularity of these trivial, repetitive stories.'

And in an article entitled 'Who's Afraid Of Enid Blyton' in 1977, Edward Blishen described Noddy as:

A wooden toy whose only positive characteristic is the uncomfortable one that his head, attached to his body by a spring, can be set nodding by anyone who cares to give it a tap. The heights of euphoria are achieved when Noddy exclaims 'Aren't people nice?' though clearly, when he is excited into this observation, he has forgotten the Giggle Goblins and all those 'horrid' characters who aren't to be made 'nice' even by a 'good spanking'.

Blishen felt saddened that Enid had been slowly poisoning the reading ability of children with her over simplified style, but put the enduring popularity of the books down to her undemanding vocabulary and plots, adding: 'Her voice bumbles in the ear like that of some universal mum, a lowest common denominator of mummishness, alternately cosy and cross.'

In the 1980s, yet again the blame was laid firmly at Enid's door for a nationwide decline in reading standards. But when a librarian called Sheila Ray published an assessment of Enid's life's work in 1982, in the wake of numerous public libraries stripping her books from their shelves, and she was forced to conclude that no other author at the time was doing more to encourage children to read – and to read right through to the end of the book. As a result of Ray's research in a book entitled *The Blyton Phenomenon*, schools and libraries gradually started to restock Enid's books and by 1991 she was listed by the Public Lending Rights as one of the most borrowed children's authors. The same year she was named by *The Sunday Times* in 1000 Makers of the Twentieth Century, a list of influential international figures.

The legacy she left was also vast in financial terms. The company she and Kenneth had set up together in 1950 to handle her business affairs, Darrell Waters Limited, was sold to the British leisure group Trocadero in 1996 for £14.6 million. Gillian remained an active board member of the new company, under the new name of Enid Blyton Limited, which was later sold on to Chorion, a company which also held majority shares in the works of various authors including Agatha Christie, Raymond Chandler and Roger Hargreaves. The deal also included copyright of all the original Noddy drawings by Harmsen van der Beek which allowed Chorion to make a sixty-five-part series for the BBC which sparked major merchandising tie-ins with magazines, toys and further books – another marketing coup for Enid.

Noddy was published in China for the first time in 2004, where publishers anticipated selling 95 million books. Chorion, owner of the Enid Blyton rights at the time, awarded the Chinese rights to the 100-part animated Noddy series to Beijing's Foreign Language Teaching and Research Press, the academic publishing arm of Beijing's Foreign Studies University. The deal included a complete roll out of Noddy books, toys and DVDs to all children under 5-years-old, based on the success of a similar deal in France where Noddy is known as Oui Oui. Similar rights were also sold to publishers in Hong Kong, Taiwan, South Korea and Malaysia, Iceland and Indonesia. Nicholas James, former chief executive of Chorion, said: 'Enid Blyton was herself a pre-school teacher and created Noddy in order to make the learning experience more fun for children, thereby increasing the character's educational value. We are confident that children in China will warmly welcome Noddy into their hearts just as they have right around the world.'

In 1982 a charitable trust was set up in her name to continue the fundraising efforts her clubs had started. Initially Imogen ran the Enid Blyton Trust For Children, with her daughter Sophie Smallwood taking over in later years.

Chapter Seventeen

E nid's fans were left reeling in 1989 when Imogen decided to write a deeply personal memoir of her own upbringing. *A Childhood At Green Hedges* starkly revealed how Enid overlooked the emotional needs of her own children because, as one of her publishers remarked: 'She was so busy being a mother to the world's children.' Imogen dared to say what many had long suspected, that Enid had been unable or unwilling to give her daughters the affection they needed growing up, leaving them with the feeling that she was 'acting' the role of mother and never felt truly comfortable around them. Enid would spend so long writing, answering letters or wandering her famous garden deep in contemplation that there was little time left for the children: 'She never truly became a mother,' Imogen wrote. 'Which of us was the more emotionally crippled I cannot tell.'

The revelations seemed to spark an open season on mocking Enid, and how old-fashioned her stories seemed to modern audiences, most notably a spate of Comic Strip TV films starring Jennifer Saunders, Dawn French and Adrian Edmondson. Their popular film *Five Go Mad In Dorset* ridiculed the wholesome language and attitudes Enid portrayed. And with her work back in the glare of the public eye in the 1990s some of Enid's former publishers bowed to immense public pressure to make changes to certain passages of her work which were considered politically incorrect or at odds with modern thinking. Portions of texts were removed which could be construed as snobbish, racist or sexist. When the *Famous Five* books were modernised, Julian and Dick started to help Anne with the housework, the word gay was changed to happy, and queer was removed entirely – Enid had used the word to describe strange people sixteen times in *Five Go Adventuring Again*. References to gypsies were altered too – In *Five Fall Into Adventure* Enid wrote that the gypsies and their caravans 'pong'. And any mention of biscuits were changed to cookies in an attempt to widen appeal to American audiences.

In other stories characters' names were changed as publishers feared close analysis could throw up yet more accusations of Enid being deemed out of touch. In *The Faraway Tree* stories Dick and Fanny were renamed

Rick and Frannie, as what were common names in the 1950s had become vulgar slang in the 1990s and would provoke sniggers from the audience. In the TV series Aunt Fanny became Aunt Frances. Dame Slap became Dame Snap, and scolded naughty children instead of spanking them. Mary and Jill of the *Adventurous Four* were updated to Pippa and Zoe, and it was decided their friend Andy who worked with his father as a fisherman should actually go to school, and in the new version the teenage boy only helped his dad at weekends.

But the biggest storm of publicity came when the golliwog owner of the Toytown garage, Mr Golly, was eventually replaced by a Mr Sparks. The story of *The Three Golliwogs* was renamed *The Three Bold Pixies* and in the updated version goblins and not golliwogs double-crossed Noddy. In the TV series a new character was introduced called Dinah Doll, who was described as 'a black assertive, ethnic minority female'. To many detractors these changes were seen as an overdue and necessary way to move with the times, but others argued it was a case of political correctness taken too far, and felt young readers should have the chance to read the original stories as Enid had intended, with the understanding that they were written in a different historical context, when attitudes were not the same.

Author Barbara Stoney argued in the *Daily Mail*:

The Famous Five are famously intrepid explorers. One adventure takes them into the dank recesses of a series of caves. Surely they shouldn't be permitted to take such unwarranted risks? What of the danger of falling rocks, hypothermia or, worse, predatory pederasts? These days, no self-respecting mother would allow four preadolescent youngsters – and their dog – to wander through subterranean caverns without responsible adult supervision, safety hats and satellite phones. Surely the errant Five should be safely at home, experiencing their adventures vicariously through their computer screens? Well, of course they shouldn't. Children, by and large, want to be thrilled and excited by stories that move ineluctably towards a happy ending. Even Blyton's sternest critics concede that her talent is to engross the most recalcitrant or tentative young reader in tales that do just that: in Blyton, the good reliably triumph and the bad are punished. It is all palpable madness. The fact is that no child has been rendered racist or sexist by reading Enid Blyton. And the greatest absurdity of all is that, to my certain knowledge, not one of those voices raised in clamorous complaint against her belongs to a child.

The debates raged on as the changes were made, although the new editions scarcely affected sales either way. The 'sanitised' versions were just as popular as the originals, and continued to sell at a rate of 6 to 7 million copies a year, in more than 40 languages around the world. Widespread use of the Internet sparked another surge in popularity, leading to the formation of a new website for the Enid Blyton Society which has a very well-attended annual Enid Blyton Day. For many years one of the society's founders also edited *Green Hedges* magazine, which was published regularly until 2002. There are still regular Enid Blyton Days held around the world, and enthusiastic collectors buy and sell rare editions of Enid's books for hundreds of pounds. In surveys of the reading tastes and habits of children between 8 and 12-years-old she is invariably shown to be among the most popular, and even if she had had a massive marketing budget to carry out systematic research to discover what children liked, she still could not have produced books more guaranteed to please that particular age group.

To mark the centenary of Enid's birth on 11 August 1997 there were a host of celebrations, including a glitzy reception at the Victoria & Albert Museum in London to announce that every year a special award would be given to someone who had contributed outstanding service to children. The award itself was a miniature silver replica of a stone statue of a child reading which Enid had at Green Hedges. Replicas of Noddy and Big Ears were installed outside Beaconsfield Town Hall, and the famous Christmas lights in London's Regent Street were devoted to celebrating her work, including illuminated versions of her famous signature. The Royal Mail issued a special set of commemorative stamps and many of Enid's best-selling books were reprinted with their original cover designs. The Queen celebrated Enid's contribution to children's literature by inviting Noddy and Mr Plod to a children's party at Buckingham Palace. Also that year a model of Green Hedges was installed at Bekonscot, the model village in Beaconsfield, to mark what an important role the house itself had played in Enid's writing, and various blue plaques were mounted at significant locations including Elfin Cottage, the first house she and Hugh had bought together. Her old school, St Christopher's in Beckenham, held a party and Gillian unveiled a plaque at Southernhay, the house in Surrey where Enid had set up a small school at the start of her working life.

And the National Centre for Research's conference on children's literature in 1997 was forced to admit that her stories were 'a thumping good read' and regardless of whether you liked them or not, Enid must be recognised for the contribution she made to literacy for young people. However, despite her constant support of the teaching profession, Enid never managed to feature as part of the National Curriculum, which would have meant young people studying her books in classrooms.

Duncan McLaren, who described himself ironically as 'the world's keenest Enid Blyton scholar', published an hilarious account of his quest to discover what had made her tick in 2007. *Looking For Enid* was a diary of a walk he embarked on with his rather baffled girlfriend around various key places that inspired Enid, including her first home in Clockhouse Road and Elfin Cottage. He suggested much of her work was full of Freudian slips and double entendres; when she was newly married for the first time she wrote *The Adventures of Binkle and Flip*, about which McLaren said: 'Most chapters start with Binkle and Flip lying in bed – no other book is anything like as bed orientated.' And when she embarked on a passionate affair with Kenneth a similar theme emerged in Enid's writing, McLaren pointed out in humorous style, adding that her work became packed with erotic symbols such as tunnels, caves, towers and lighthouses. *The Wonderful Torch* was described as 'A lovely one, about eight inches long, which went on and off when he pushed the knob up and down.'

Many devoted fans have explored the coastal areas of Dorset that so inspired Enid, and a number of books have been published on this theme – *The Dorset Days of Enid Blyton*, by Vivienne Endecott in 2002 and *Enid Blyton and her Enchantment With Dorset* by Andrew Norman in 2005. In 2008 there was another spate of fury among literary circles when Enid topped a nationwide poll of favourite authors, beating even Jane Austen and Charles Dickens to the top spot. Roald Dahl was second and J.K. Rowling came third. The Costa Book Awards asked 2,000 adults to name their most loved writers, but when the results were announced, writer Anthony Horowitz complained in the *Daily Telegraph* that British people were 'being asked to genuflect in front of a fossil', while children's author Philip Pullman compared Enid's stories to 'mechanically recovered meat'. But Jeff Norton of Chorion, Enid's publisher, said: 'Her storytelling is timeless and this result confirms that her books are still a firm favourite today. What makes Blyton so successful is her imaginative, exciting and magical style. Her writing has sent countless young readers on thrilling adventures.'

In 2009 Enid's granddaughter Sophie Smallwood wrote the first new Noddy adventure in forty-five years, called *Noddy and The Farmyard Muddle*. Sophie, a primary school teacher from West Sussex who never met Enid, said: 'I'm not trying to write a brand new Noddy book, I'm trying to write something in her honour. It would be bad to have written something that was totally modern and totally unfamiliar.' Sophie said she wanted to remain true to the original stories as far as possible but decided to banish golliwogs from the new story in a bid to avoid any further controversy:

> When I was a child I wasn't aware there was a negative attitude to them. It says more about the people who made these comments than it does about the books. They were missing the point because these books were all for children, and children do not see it at that level at all. Most people now realise the toys removed from the stories were just toys, but sometimes things are just too complicated. I thought it would cause more upset to recreate something that had moved on.

The new adventure focused instead on a wooden elf who tried to solve mysterious events which coincided with the arrival of the goblins. Fans welcomed the new tale but some felt the removal of the golliwogs was unnecessary as they were a product of their time. Tony Summerfield from the Enid Blyton Society told the *Daily Mail*:

> I don't think when Enid wrote about golliwogs there was anything racist in it at all. Gollies were just ordinary nursery toys and it wasn't until much later that they became seen as racist symbols, but even then it was only by a vociferous minority. I can understand that the publishers are aiming it at children and don't want to do anything controversial, but I do think they underestimate children, who should be able to understand that they were written in a historical context.

The book was illustrated by Robert Tyndall who had actually painted many of the watercolours for the original series in the 1950s, he said:

> Noddy is made of wood but he eats cakes and jellies and drinks ginger beer and does all sorts of things he shouldn't be able to do. I like the goblins and what they represent, which is a challenge to established order. There's something very basic about Noddy, which I don't try to analyse too much for fear of destroying it. When I was a child, I used to take toys to pieces and when I tried to put them together again there were always parts left over. And that taught me a lesson to not just take things apart.

Disney launched a new cartoon series called *Famous Five: On The Case* in 2008 which featured a cast made up of the children of the original characters that Enid created. Anne had grown up, moved to California after college and had a daughter, Allie, who loved shopping and texting, while George's daughter was an Indian character called Jo, short for Jyoti, a Hindi name meaning light. Apparently George had her daughter after meeting her husband Ravi while she was trekking in the Himalayas before settling down as a botanist in the fictional Dorset town of Falcongate. Max was the son of another of the original characters Julian, and was outgoing, athletic and enjoyed thrill-seeking activities such as surfing in Cornwall. Dick's son Dylan was a business tycoon who carried a laptop and video camera at all times. Expressions such as gosh, golly and super were replaced as they discovered a factory selling pirate DVDs in the first episode. Enid would hardly have understood a word of the modern day script but Jeff Norton of Chorion said: 'We wanted to keep the essence of Blyton's stories. These characters do solve crimes and there is danger. Often they start their adventures like in the books by going on a bicycle ride or sailing.' A Disney spokesman added:

> The new characters are smart kids that love to get down and dirty in the outdoors. And one of the things I am particularly proud of is a 'how to' section at the end of each show which gives viewers tips on doing something they have seen the *Five* doing – like sailing. Many children, particularly city dwellers, don't go out and do these kind of activities. So much of the original fun happened outdoors and we wanted to promote that.

Chorion released new editions of *The Wishing Chair* and *Malory Towers* series in 2008 as part of an ambitious plan to boost the brand, which was already making over £200 million a year in sales. Jeff Norton, senior vice president of brand development said: 'A lot of children don't know that Enid Blyton isn't a living author. And frankly, they don't care. She's the author of books they love.' Sequels to the *Malory Towers* series were published in Germany and a French author called Claude Voilier added new stories to the *Famous Five* series, which were later translated into English. Between 1999 and 2001 writer Anne Digby continued the *Naughtiest Girl in the School* too.

In the US Noddy was becoming almost as popular as the programme *Sesame Street*, and he was even invited to ring the bell to launch the day's trading at the New York Stock Exchange. A new exhibition of Noddy art in London and a 3D CGI stage show called *Noddy in Toyland* hit the West

End stage. Actress Sienna Miller and her fashion designer sister Savannah, who own the clothing label Twenty8Twelve unveiled a collection of Noddy-themed styles at London Fashion Week in 2009. Savannah explained that she had been particularly inspired by Big Ears' 'blue swing jacket and cropped cream trousers with the green stripe'.

A much-anticipated screen biography of Enid's life was screened on BBC4 in 2009, starring Helena Bonham Carter. She was portrayed as always looking immaculate with her trademark bright-red lipstick, but a rather melodramatic, and often dark character who presented her public and her family with very different faces. Treating her children and staff with icy coldness and a lack of sympathy, the character was unfailingly warm and affectionate to her young readers. The producer of *Enid,* Lee Morris, explained: 'She was dedicated to her fans, she did her best to write back to all of them. Her relationship with her children, on the other hand, was quite distant. Her fans were her real family.' In the film Enid was intolerant of her first husband, and she was seen seamlessly erasing Hugh from her life and moving Kenneth in with a ruthless efficiency, and then blocking Hugh's attempts to see his children: 'It would have caused a huge scandal,' added Morris. 'Today it would have been uncovered, but it was different then. She did the deal with her first husband, but then made it very hard for him to see his daughters.'

Helena Bonham Carter showed a cynical and manipulative side to Enid, constantly reinventing herself and concealing the truth to maintain her brand. The actress explained:

> She was emotionally immature. She's a therapist's dream. She retreated to a place where life was lovely and carried on creating that world. She didn't want to deal with anything that interrupted it. In her personal life she was cruel by accident because that's what she needed to keep herself afloat. Hilariously, and almost insanely, she reinvented facts that she didn't like. She just wanted to carry on creating this fantastic world that, actually, millions of others wanted to escape to because it was so convincing. She was allergic to reality – if there was something she didn't like then she either ignored it or rewrote her life. Enid's self awareness was brilliant and she was incredibly controlling too. I was attracted to the role because she was bonkers. She was an emotional mess and quite barking mad. Enid said that she thought as a child and wrote as a child. She was a forever child. I had a quote on the front of my script which I

think was the key to playing her. It says growing old is compulsory, but growing up is optional. That was her. She was unbelievably modern. She was a complete workaholic, an achievement junkie and an extremely canny businesswoman. She knew how to brand herself, right down to the famous signature.

Director James Hawes confirmed that Enid never fully recovered from her father leaving: 'Her success, and what was wrong with her life, seem to come from exactly the same place. This is armchair psychology, but she did in some way come to an emotional halt at that point and some part of her stayed forever young. She was incredibly business-efficient. If she wanted to get a point across or to do a deal there was an icy authority about her.'

Enid's youngest daughter approved the script before the film went into production, and the shoot in Surrey took just two weeks. The cast and crew were nervous when Imogen, at the age of 74, decided to pay a visit to the set: 'I was really worried about it – we all were,' admitted Lee Morris. She watched a scene between Helena Bonham Carter and Matthew MacFadyen who played her father Hugh. 'It was a tense moment because she was walking into a drawing room in which two people were playing her mum and dad. She spoke to Matthew and to Helena, watched them work, then told us she was reassured. Not only that, she then spent the afternoon giving us some really useful advice.' Imogen pointed out that Enid insisted all her maids addressed her as Mrs Pollock, not Mrs Blyton, and the script was altered accordingly.

To mark the seventieth anniversary of the *Famous Five* in 2012, an Enid Blyton Day was held. As part of this the Famous Five Adventure Trail was launched, which takes in some of the Dorset locations that crop up in the stories, such as Corfe Castle which was the inspiration for Kirrin Castle, where the gang discovered gold ingots in the dungeon in *Five On A Treasure Island*, their very first adventure. Describing it, Enid wrote: 'On a low hill rose the ruined castle. It had been built of big white stones. Broken archways, tumbledown towers, ruined walls – that was all there was left of a once beautiful castle, proud and strong, now the jackdaws nested in it.' It also includes Brownsea Island which appeared as Whispering Island in *Five Have a Mystery To Solve* (1962), and Manor Farm in Stourton Caundle near Dorchester which inspired *Five Go To Finniston Farm* (1960). The heathland from *Five Go To Mystery Moor* (1954) was drawn from Hartland Moor near Corfe Castle, which Enid's daughter Gillian remembered visiting many years earlier: 'A lot of the natural life that Mother described in these books is very much Dorset. It's the birds, the gorse, the heather. We climbed the hill and sat in the castle, where we saw brambles growing through the flags of the courtyard and heard jackdaws calling.'

At this time most of the *Famous Five* books were reissued with new cover designs by well-known current illustrators including Quentin Blake, and Tony Ross also added his distinctive drawings to new editions of the *Secret Seven* books, which had never been out of print since 1949. The text of the *Secret Seven* stories was also given an overhaul when it was updated for twenty-first-century children. The tales about Peter, Janet, Jack, Colin, George, Pam and Barbara remained the same but much of the language was modernised, removing phrases including jolly japes, golly gosh, mercy me, guffaw and cripes. The word jersey was replaced with jumper, frocks became dresses, mother and father were changed to mum and dad, fellow to man and peculiar to strange. The aim was to help young readers in contemporary society to relate more easily to the characters. Marlene Johnson of publisher Hachette explained: 'We modernised *Famous Five* amid much murmuring. But these days you don't talk of jolly japes to kids.'

The publisher insisted that Enid's famous catchphrase 'lashings of ginger beer' must stay in the new version, but the series brand owner Chorion feared that the outdated language was preventing parents from buying the books for their children, and believed the demand could be even greater if they were more accessible: 'The magic of Blyton is the ability she has to transport readers into another world and pull them along through page turning adventure. For a lot of today's readers, that just wasn't happening because of a few outdated words and phrases, so we feel it's absolutely right to do this,' said a statement from Chorion. Anne McNeil, publishing director at Hodder, backed the changes saying: 'Very subtle changes have been made to remove the barriers that stood between the reader and the story. We have not introduced any slang or colloquial language that would place the characters in today's world.'

But the Hachette Children's Group was later forced to admit the further changes had not been necessary and performed a U-turn as many of the alterations proved so unpopular with readers. A spokesman explained:

> Essentially we were looking at dialogue and making sure it worked for a contemporary audience. It was a very subtle change and thoroughly researched but proved very unpopular. We thought it was a necessary step but it wasn't. So we are reverting to the extant classic text. The core values of Enid Blyton remain as strong as

they ever were. She believed in children, their ability to hold true friendships, their sense of adventure and their integrity. Phrases like jolly japes have come into the canon of terminology used about Enid Blyton: a shorthand for her wonderful sense of fun and humour.

As recently as 2013 the Beaconsfield Society attempted to organise a week-long celebration of Enid Blyton's life and work in her former home town, but they were faced with fierce opposition from critics who continued to brand her books racist and sexist. There were plans to erect a plaque where Green Hedges had stood, before being demolished in the early 1970s and replaced with a small estate of houses called Blyton Close. For years after she died children from all over the world continued to send letters to Green Hedges in Beaconsfield, which had been her home for thirty years. One of the campaigners against the festival, Anthony Mealing, argued: 'The moral of one of the stories is: "Don't leave any money around if there are any black children about as they will steal it." She was anti-Semitic and very racist. People don't believe me because she is too high an icon but she was.' But the co-ordinator of the event, former librarian Kari Dorme, insisted:

> In the early 1990's, some of her publishers made certain text changes – mostly to bring her stories into line with modern thought and sensitivities, particularly with regard to what some construed as snobbish, racist or sexist attitudes. Even names were modernised. You have to accept them in the time in which they were written, which was at least sixty years ago. Her books still sell at a rate of six to seven million copies a year, in more than forty languages. Enid Blyton is a marvellous story teller – a real page turner.

A few months later, a major exhibition entitled 'Mystery, Magic and Midnight Feasts: the Many Adventures of Enid Blyton' toured around Britain. It recreated Kirrin Castle, the Common Room in *Mallory Towers*, the *Secret Seven* shed and children even had the chance to sit in Noddy's car and slide down from *The Magic Far Away Tree*. There was only one mention of the golliwogs, who were referred to as gollies, with the explanation that they are now an unacceptable racial stereotype. The display also included previously unseen pages from Enid's diaries, as well as the unpublished typescript of 'Mr Tumpy's Caravan', which was only discovered shortly before the opening, when a haul of her belongings was sold at auction in 2010, following Gillian's death three years earlier. The previously unseen, dusty, yellowing 180-page manuscript tells the story of a magical caravan and the travels of its inhabitants Muffin, Puffin and a dog called Bun-Dorg. It is not known why it was never published, but the address on it was Old Thatch, her home before Green Hedges, and it appeared to be one of Enid's earliest works and may have been rejected when she was struggling to find publishers. In 1949 Enid had published a book of cartoon strips called *Tumpy and His Caravan* but they included completely different stories and characters, and Imogen thought the story may have been written towards the end of Enid's life when her dementia meant her work was clumsy and littered with mistakes. She said:

> I think it was not published because it wasn't up to her old standard. She was getting very confused. My daughter and I both think this one page that we've got shows a lot of effort, rather than the absolute free flow that came from her fingers to her typewriter in those old days when she wrote several thousand words a day.

It was hidden among a collection of seven draft manuscripts bought for £40,000 by the Seven Stories children's book centre in Newcastle. Archivist Hannah Green discovered the manuscript when she archived the collection. She said: 'It doesn't often happen that you have something unpublished by such a well known author. I think I am probably the first person, certainly in a very long time, to have read the whole thing. It's quite a surreal book, but very funny and entertaining. And very original, as a lot of her fantasy novels were.'

Another successful auction the following year saw the sale of a valuable collection of Harmsen van der Beek's original watercolour paintings of Noddy which fetched over £1,000 each. The vast collection of memorabilia belonged to the bookseller Thomas Schuster who spent eighteen years scouring fairs for items including toys and models worth around £50,000. The original Noddy car, based on a 1969 Fiat Gamine Vagnale, sold at auction in July 2013 for £29,325, with the number plate NOD513, proving that Noddy nostalgia was still as strong as ever.

Gillian died in 2007 at the age of 75, leaving an estate which included dozens of her mother's original manuscripts and annotated books, valued at over £800,000. But long-running and increasingly bitter legal wrangles meant none of the beneficiaries of her will received a penny for years. Four of Enid's six great-grandchildren, who were each left £50,000 by Gillian, launched a High Court action against two trustees of the estate, claiming they mishandled their grandmother's complicated financial affairs and reduced the value of her estate. The four children, who were set to inherit the money when they turned 25, were supported by their father David Lane, married to Gillian's daughter Sara. Their High Court writ, a copy of which was obtained by the *Mail on Sunday*, stated that property which used to belong to Enid had been sold for a fraction of its true value.

Gillian had owned several of Enid's most valuable items, including seventeen original manuscripts, forty-seven annotated or autographed books and a portrait by acclaimed artist Aubrey Claude Davidson-Houston, as well as some of her mink and leopard skin coats. Many items were sold at auction but the legal case meant there were long delays in payments to Gillian's beneficiaries. She left £100,000 to her son Owain and £50,000 to each of her grandchildren, including the four Lane children, but neither David Lane nor his wife Sara were listed in the will. Gillian also wanted £50,000 to go to the Bolton Abbey Priory near her former home in Ilkley, West Yorkshire, and the education department at the University of St Andrews where she had been a student. Once the case was eventually settled, actress Joanna Lumley added her support, saying: 'The days of Blyton bashing are over. We have taken our foot off the education pedal and I don't think it makes anyone happy. I would like to see children involved in hearty sounding pursuits such as building a camp. Or getting an entire school to go and work in a farm, for a term, all together.'

There were other surprising supporters too, an Asian literary critic called Sweta Rana wrote a passionate defence of Enid's books, saying:

> From what I've been told of Blyton, it sounds like she wasn't a very nice person. I'm a brown skinned woman who has never once made jam, so ol' Enid probably wouldn't have given me the time of day, but screw her – it's her books I care about. Her stories are simple, straightforward, and for all their dubious personal biases, there are some universally applicable messages. I never liked the golliwogs, or The Little Black Doll, and I never will. Even as a young reader they were appalling. Certain Blyton creations make me shudder; but I will defend the others. They are the diamonds in the rough, the stories that shaped my childhood. The Famous Five could have been any mix of genders, skin tones and species as far as I'm concerned. They still emboldened me with their daring escapades.

Even as a kid I knew to take these tales as loose metaphors, not as rigid fact or gospel. And the basic messages of Enid Blyton – remember that hard work pays off, be truthful and kind, strive to do good by your family and friends – those messages are universal. They transcend even Blyton's own entrenched prejudices, and apply to people of any race, gender or country.

Award-winning film star Kate Winslet signed a deal to read Enid Blyton stories for a series of talking books, and *James Bond* director Sam Mendes snapped up the film rights for *The Enchanted Wood, The Magic Faraway Tree, The Folk of The Faraway Tree* and *Up The Faraway Tree*. Shortly afterwards Old Thatch, the picturesque 'fairy tale house' where Enid was inspired to write the series, was put up for sale for £1,750,000. In 2016 a series of 96-page books parodying the originals called *Enid Blyton Books for Grown Ups* was launched, following the success of the spoof Ladybird *Books for Adults*. The ironic reinvention of Enid's classic stories saw the *Famous Five* embarking on far less innocent adventures including investigating illicit sexual liaisons and going on a gluten free diet. Titles included *Five Go On A Strategy Away Day, Five Go Parenting* and *Five Give Up The Booze*, but critics feared the books, written by humourist Bruno Vincent, could damage Enid's legacy, especially when the recently published parody *Five on Brexit Island* sold more than 372,000 copies.

The same year the owner of an Enid Blyton gift shop in Dorset was banned from displaying tea towels featuring golliwogs in her shop window. Viv Endecott argued that she had sold thousands of rag dolls from her shop called Ginger Pop in Purbeck:

It is about time the English started celebrating our culture. The golliwog is part of our culture and no one needs to be offended by it. You cannot ban bits of history you don't like, history is part of our country. I sell thousands upon thousands of golliwogs in the shop every year. There are so few places to get one these days because most people are too frightened to sell them.

New technology in 2000 meant it was possible to create a computer generated series of *Noddy*, with 100 episodes being shown on both sides of the Atlantic. *Noddy Live* sold out arenas and stadiums across the country, and a language teaching programme called *Say It With Noddy* introduced a new generation of young children to languages as diverse as Mandarin and Swahili.

Former children's laureate Anne Fine explained:

> Though Enid Blyton's work is still just as easy to criticise on grounds of literary quality, we have become infinitely more grateful for sheer readability in our children's authors. In times of failing reading levels and limitless other distractions, we grasp at any author who has that turn-the-page quality. And for reasons that may remain entirely mysterious to reading adults, she certainly has that.

Chapter Eighteen

The enduring affection that millions of people, young and old, continue to feel for both the stories and Enid herself is a remarkable testament to how ingrained she has become into the culture and tradition of many societies. Big Ears and Mr Plod are still commonly used nicknames, and the expression 'lashings of ginger beer' needs little explanation for those of us who use it to indicate great excitement about an upcoming picnic or feast. Of course she still has her critics, and many remain as derisory as ever about Enid's books for various different reasons, but more often mention of them is met with amusement and pangs of nostalgia than mockery or anger. Just the sight of her famous signature will conjure up happy memories of childhood reading and escapism. Enid gave millions of children their first taste of literature and encouraged a love of reading. She remains a household name, certainly in Britain, with easily understood references to her stories found in mass media, popular culture, news items or high-brow commentary that often have nothing to do with her work at all.

Whether Enid is considered a good role model or a bad influence, she had a Trojan work ethic, which was truly astonishing until she could not physically continue. She felt she owed it to her readers to provide them not only with more stories but also to ensure they only knew of the sunny, happy world she crafted for them so carefully. When Imogen explored her mother's emotional flaws, she seemed forgiving and suggested that it was not Enid's fault that she was unable to be the parent she longed for: 'I am only sure that these handicaps are a legacy of childhood and that they are passed down the generations as if a physical familial disease is present,' Imogen wrote.

The literary critic Philip Thody damned Enid as 'depressingly normal' but as we have seen she was very far from that. The sheer volume of the work she created made her extraordinary for a start, and her deeply complex psychology revealed she was an exceptionally unusual woman. No doubt the early loss of her father shaped her emotional make-up, and drove her to work with such a fervent zeal. Her boarding school stories reveal how disenchanted she was with her own mother and longed to escape the confines and suffocating restrictions of her suburban home. She exposed more of herself in the creation of George, the tomboy heroine of the *Famous Five* series, who was clearly rooted in her own personality. Like George, Enid appeared to have a fierce and tough exterior, ready to take on the world, but deep down she was sensitive and vulnerable. As Enid herself said: 'Even if you have never met me, you know me very well because you have read so many books of mine. I am sure that you know exactly what I stand for, and the things I believe in, without any doubt at all.'

Author of *Enid Blyton and the Mystery of Children's Literature* David Rudd argued that Enid continued to remain so compelling because she wrote like the oral storytellers of fairy tales which have been passed down through generations, with the listener making up extra details as they go along: 'To my mind that gets at the essence of what Blyton was doing. And why she worked so cross culturally. Although it's obviously set in a mythical middle–class England, it's so skeletal and schematic. It's like fairy tales – there are just bare outlines and people imported their own colouring and filled it out.' He went on to argue that the changes made to modernise Enid's stories could be seen as adults interfering in a world created specifically for children:

> It's in danger of killing the goose with the golden egg. She's often said to have a limited vocabulary, and it strikes me as ironic that they've actually made it more limited. The word 'becalmed' was used in a Noddy work and it has been changed to 'isn't moving.' Why does a writer accused of being middle class, snobbish, sexist, racist continue to fascinate in our multicultural world? To fascinate not only in France, Germany and Australia, but also Malaysia, Russia and Japan, and in languages such as Catalan and Tamil?

Critic Robert Leeson paid tribute to Enid saying:

> She absorbed the world of children and gave it back to them. Her first writings were directly for the children she taught. As someone said of her, 'she knew just how children like a story to be.' That was the ace in her pack. She started them young: no complaints about the customer from her. She fed the children, from four to fourteen, on themselves. She satisfied them and left them hungry for more of the same.

Many of her fans and critics alike – and both have been equally vocal over the years – agree that the key reason she wrote for children of all ages was so they could grow up with her. Toddlers would begin by listening to the enduringly popular *Noddy* tales, then go on to read the exciting fantasy and adventure stories for themselves. By writing series she ensured her loyal readers stayed with her for years, unable to resist the temptation of the next instalment and eagerly wanting to know what would happen to their favourite characters next. Generally girls have tended to stick with Enid longer than boys because the boarding school stories appealed to them more. All the stories struck a chord with children, chapters usually ended on a high note or exciting cliff hanger which led her work to be considered the pre-cursor to the modern soap operas of today, back in a time when there was very little mainstream television for children. Ahead of her time, Enid was keenly aware of the importance of branding, insisting that her distinctive signature was on the front of every book, and she famously did not listen to critics above the age of 12. She understood her readers far better than any expert market research or expensive focus groups could have explained. Childlike herself, she knew that young people enjoyed the familiarity of sequels and, like them or not, she churned them out at an impressive rate. At the peak of her productivity she would write up to 8,000 words a day, and if her mind had not been cruelly ravaged by senile dementia the number of books with her famous signature on them would surely be in the thousands. She once remarked that she 'Could write a whole book in one sitting if only I didn't have to eat or sleep.' It all started with her first book, a slim volume of poetry called *Child Whispers*, in 1922, and she went on to publish more than 800 titles before her death in 1968.

For Enid, stories were a way to escape, and much of her best writing was done at the most difficult times of her life. As a child Enid's mother had taught her to hide from reality, and she translated that into an imaginary world where she could escape any time she needed it. When she was happy however, as she was during her later years with Kenneth, Enid did not need to run away and found it much more difficult to come up with fresh ideas. As a result her stories became repetitive during periods of contentment, and much more exciting and mysterious when she needed a safe place to hide.

Even at the height of her confidence, when she was wealthier and more successful than she ever dreamt of, Enid could not have predicted the enormous audience she would eventually reach. For most of the twentieth century she was the most popular children's author in Britain, and was famous around the world. But despite her enormous popularity and her prolific output, no other writer in the history of children's literature has ever provoked such a furious backlash, or aroused such strongly held opinions. She encountered fierce hostility and has been dismissed as irrelevant and mind numbing and yet generations of children would beg to differ. The stories are as widely adored now as they were decades ago and continue to sell at the astonishing rate of one a minute in Britain, and we have seen the reasons behind her remarkable success.

The childlike wonder that never left her allowed Enid to relate so successfully to children; she knew they wanted secrets, adventures and environments in which adults had very minor roles to play – adults tended to be villains or the ones to ruin all the fun. She understood how children were fascinated by remote locations such as caves or islands; indeed her first full-length adventure story was called *The Secret Island* while the first titles in two of her most popular series were *The Island of Adventure* and *Five on a Treasure Island*. Children had freedom to roam, far from home and often for days at a time. They could embark on dangerous adventures without grown-ups telling them not to. Animals were hugely important too, inspired by Enid's own love of wildlife, they often had human qualities and great emphasis was placed on being kind to them. Honesty and good behaviour were always rewarded in her stories, while lying and cheating were punished, but the stories always ended happily.

Like it or not, there has always been something about the relentless nature of Enid's work, the sheer volume of it, that meant she has managed to win her adversaries round. Even decades after her death she remained as much of an unstoppable force as she had been at her peak. It is difficult to argue against the merits of the work given such a vast and loyal following. Her popularity has fluctuated many times, but she still remains in the top ten most borrowed children's authors, despite some stiff competition from phenomenally popular modern writers such as J.K. Rowling – who came up with the popular *Harry Potter* series about children developing at boarding school. And over the years scores of popular writers have talked about how inspired they were by Enid to follow in her footsteps, and many have unashamedly acknowledged their early love of Blyton. But despite her huge and diverse global fan base, no other author has been as widely and consistently attacked to the extent that Enid has been since the early 1950s. Even adults who are not particularly against her work, or the idea of their children reading the stories, are well aware of the underlying criticism. But ever since children started reading for pleasure, adults have tried to ban some of their favourite books believing they are unsuitable for one reason or another. As far back as 1568 the schoolmaster Roger Ascham lobbied against Malory's *Morte d'Arthur* and 200 years later *Robinson Crusoe* was attacked for fear the reading of it might lead to 'an early taste for the rambling life'. *Robin Hood* was widely condemned, and at the start of the nineteenth century, *Cinderella* came under fire for containing 'envy, jealousy, a dislike to mothers-in-law and half-sisters, vanity and a love of dress'.

Many literary critics, psychologists and parents have struggled to understand Enid's enduring appeal, and the most common explanation is that she never really left her childhood behind. Her connection to her early years gave Enid a unique ability to continue to relate to young people throughout her adult life. She became as excited about the stories as her readers did, which meant they devoured each page with the same level of excitement as she appeared to write them. The stories may have been simplistic, but to Enid that straightforward world was certainly preferable to some of the more unpleasant aspects of adult life. Burying herself safely in the familiar enchanted world of her own imagination allowed her to easily block out the harsh realities of life, which she found so hard to accept. Rereading Enid's original work today, it is important to remember that she was born and grew up in a time when attitudes were so very different. She was influenced by ideas that were commonly held when she was young, and which are certainly considered outdated and inappropriate now. Some of the language she used, rightly condemned for being racist, was familiar at a time before the Second World War when there were very few people of different ethnic backgrounds living in rural Britain. In the 1930s the British Empire was a powerful global force. Enid was also accused of sexism and snobbishness, but in her orbit gender roles were much more defined for boys and girls than they are now. Boys were encouraged to be brave and adventurous while girls were expected to help with domestic duties, something that she rebelled strongly against as a young tomboy herself, but nevertheless gender stereotyping would have influenced her thinking. What concerned Enid above all was good storytelling for children. And Enid's books have not only survived but thrived. Times have certainly changed, but her books are still bought and enjoyed by children all over the world and she remains among the top-selling children's authors of all time.

As Enid herself was fond of saying: 'Writing for children is an art in itself, and a most interesting one.'

Index